# Faith Alone:

## Stories of an Amazing Dog

# Faith Alone:

## Stories of an Amazing Dog

Jude Stringfellow

To order additional copies of this book, contact:
Xlibris Corporation
1-888-795-4274
www.Xlibris.com
Orders@Xlibris.com
35355

Disclaimer

Some of the names in this book were changed at the request of the person whose name was changed, or because it was the right thing to do. Matrix's name really is Matrix, and he really is *my* dog, and he really is perfect . . . perfect in every way.

# Contents

To Matrix—*my* dog

3 John 1:13-14

*"For I had many things to write to you, but I will not do so with pen and ink. Soon we will see each other face to face and we will talk. Our friends greet you—Greet our friends with a kiss."*

*Credits:*

Photos of Faith and my family were taken by myself, Stephen Holman of ***Zuma Press*** and Peyton Stovall of the Edmond Outlook. Stephen Holman is Faith's personal photographer, having had the opportunity to shoot pictures for several occasions including the Tulsa World, National Geographic for Kids, and other professional magazines and newspapers interested in Faith. Stephen resides in Tulsa, Oklahoma. Peyton is a freelance photojournalist who works with the popular ***magazine Edmond Outlook*** in Edmond, Oklahoma.

Faith and I want to say hello to our little cousin Kaleigh Benton in Siloam Springs, Arkansas. Kaleigh had a friend or two that didn't quite believe she was Faith's cousin, but she is—so this should settle the matter once and for all. We love you Kaleigh, kiss your mom Mandi, you Aunt Angie, your Grandma Janelle and your Grandpa Ron for us.

# Introduction

I have told this story over and over again whenever I am in the store talking with someone who may recognize me from being on a television show or in a newspaper or magazine with my dog Faith. Seemingly, the story begins, it has a middle, and usually all too often, it has a quick ending as I'm checking out and have to run. This time, I get the opportunity to sit down and explain to everyone the miracle that is my dog Faith. She isn't normal, she isn't average, she isn't anything short of a real living miracle that God decided I needed. He was right. At the time Faith came into my life, our lives, we were just getting over a terrible family situation and there was hurt and heartache still lingering around our daily lives. We were sad at times, happy at times, but always wondering if we were going to be a healed family or if we would just have to try and make due with what we had. So many families face this situation. It's hard to start a new routine, or to try and put away the sad things that are happening in your life. It's difficult to try and find the time to change what is hurting in your life in order to make your family get along. So often teenagers don't want to talk to their parents about what is hurting them. It's hard for parents to stop what they are doing because they have to work, or they have to pay bills. We didn't want to end up in a sad family—we had to find a way to help ourselves, and for us that meant taking care of Faith.

Thank God for Faith. The day she came into my house I wasn't thinking that, but it soon became apparent to me that she would be the one thing we really needed. It gave us a chance as a family to forget about our own problems and to concentrate on her. Faith was never normal. She wasn't born normally or into a normal happy family, and she would never be considered an average dog. She had severe physical problems to overcome and she couldn't do it alone. Her situation reminded me of the fact that I had pretty bad problems going on in my family and I wasn't able to completely overcome any of them by myself either. So maybe, I thought, maybe if I can just pour all of my energy into helping this little dog to learn how to be more normal, more average, it will help me to forget about my sad days and I can become at least a more tolerant person. Little did I know. She would completely change not only my life, but my children's lives, and many many lives around the world. All because she did what she was suppose to do, and that would be to walk by faith.

When my son Reuben (We call him Reu) brought Faith to me she wasn't named. She was just a little fuzzy, yellow, dirty, mess of a dog and she lay in his hand almost without movement. She was sick, she was hurt, she was anything but desirable. If you were to go out and pick a puppy from a litter she would certainly not be the one you would choose. Surely you would have to notice like I did, that she didn't have a front right leg. It wasn't there. It simply wasn't there. Next, her left front leg was bent all the way backward and was sort of flopped over her left shoulder. Almost like a broken Barbie doll, or even like a baby seal. I remember my son asking if we could bend it back. I silently thought to myself "I wish I could", but I knew it was not a possibility.

Besides being hurt or deformed the little puppy was really stinky. She had been laying in or rolling in poo and she had matted hair with nasty clumps of poo and hair everywhere. She looked and smelled really badly. Then something happened. She raised her head from my son's palm. She was so small her entire body actually fit inside his hand. She lifted up her head and she turned it, she looked up, straight at me. She didn't cry because her voice box was affected. She couldn't make a sound. She just looked at me. She blinked, and she stared. The look in those big, puppy, brown eyes was so strong and so amazing I couldn't turn my face from her. She was speaking to me through her eyes as if to say "I can't do this. I can't make it. Will you help me?" I don't know if I answered her out loud, but I know my heart was forever changed. I couldn't say no. I couldn't possibly say no. From the moment she asked me, I was her captive.

We called her "Yellow Dog" before she actually had a name. We didn't know exactly what we wanted to call her and therefore didn't give her a real name until after we thought about all of the possibilities. Naming something is very important to us, we usually come up with several names and then dwindle it down to one. My daughter Caity wanted to name her Miracle or Princess, but Princess was her mother's name. Reu wanted to call her Grace I think, and I know I was thinking of naming her D'og which is actually pronounced D-o-g. I believe it was Laura who said "Well God worked a miracle by making her in the first place, but if she actually walks it would have to be by faith, so we could call her Faith." Well, I still called her Yellow Dog, and still do when it's just she and I. She doesn't mind and I'm 100% sure she knows her real name because everywhere we go people call out to her. "Faith!" "Faith!" and she'll turn and give them a really big doggie, tongue-wagging smile.

I say she's not normal because she doesn't have four legs, but she is normal in most other dog ways. She will chase a rabbit in the fields behind our house, or the squirrel that lives in the tree outside the front door. She'll go to Dolese Park and think nothing of chasing the geese and ducks right into the water! Laura has jumped into the water a number of times to save Faith because, believe it or not, Faith doesn't swim as well as other dogs do. She can swim, but it's not pretty. I'll tell you more about that in another chapter. We wanted our puppy to be as normal as possible, and that was going to take a lot more than work, it was going to take a little faith too.

# Chapter One

## Before Faith

Reuben was fifteen and a half years old when he decided to pull my car out of the garage and warm it up for me. Novembers can be warm in Oklahoma, but this Sunday morning was a bit nippy, just cold enough to make a boy decide to warm up his mother's car. The weather gave Reu all the excuses he needed to pull the car out, warm it up and surprise Mom before she drove the family to church. Wow, looking back I have to say—I was surprised. I was in the bathroom putting on the last touches of my makeup. The girls had for some reason, decided they didn't want to go to church that morning, and this actually turned out to be a good thing. Sometimes when the girls have stayed up all night on the internet, or when they've been talking on the phone without permission, they are far too tired to get up in the mornings and get ready to go with me to church. Had either of them been awake they would have probably been in the kitchen eating a bowl of cereal or going through the refrigerator to find a string cheese to wolf down before taking off. If that had been the case they could have (and probably would have) been hurt when the car Reu had pulled out into the driveway suddenly came slamming through the kitchen wall with a very loud bang. It came through the house knocking the heavy refrigerator several feet across the kitchen floor. "What was that?" I remember screaming out. What the heck was that terrible noise? I ran from the bathroom, around the living room, and found the front end of my car, or what looked like the front end of my car, in the kitchen. The walls were busted out, something white was sticking out of the massive hole, and my refrigerator was blocking my way to the garage to see what had happened. I knew it had to be Reuben because my girls were still in bed. I don't think they even woke up when the wall exploded.

I managed to get around the fridge and past the garage door. Immediately I was sprayed with what seemed like hundreds gallons of water coming from the obviously smashed-in washing machine. It hadn't been my car's nose that crashed through the wall after all. It was my washer. My dryer wasn't in any better shape. Though the washer had a car-sized hole in the front of it, the dryer had been slammed by the washer and into the beams of the kitchen wall. Water was everywhere! My car was white like my refrigerator, the washer, the dryer, and even the paint on the kitchen walls. All I could see were layers of white paint, beams, machines, and what I assumed was my son, probably crumpled up in the middle of all of it. I could hear the car's motor running. I couldn't quite get over the top of it to get to the driver's seat and the wheels were spinning. I was actually afraid to go around behind the car to get to my son, but I did do exactly that. When I got to the front of the car he wasn't in the car. My son was gone. Where was my son? Water still spraying and making it hard to see and work through the mess. It was just cold enough to be a real problem and I remember thinking I was about to freeze to death out in my garage. I know I was screaming his name, but he wasn't answering me.

About a minute passed and I found him. He was on the porch of the house crying with his hands over his head. He was rocking back and forth and saying he was sorry. If I was cold I forgot that I was. Immediately I checked Reu to be sure he was OK. He seemed to be upset, but in one piece. I trekked back to the garage to turn the car off, I could at least do that. I couldn't stop the water, I couldn't pull the car out, but I could turn it off. I held my boy and I asked him over and over if he was OK. Yes, he told me, he was OK, but the car—he was so upset about the car. I wondered if he even knew what he had done to every one of my appliances.

After a few minutes an elderly neighbor who had heard the noise, came out to investigate. She got her husband to go to the water valve and to turn it off at the main. He had a key. I was so happy to see that as my entire garage was about six inches under water by this point. Taking Reu to the hospital was going to be a challenge as we first had to get the car out of the washing machine. We did, and upon arriving at the hospital for an examination my son turned to me and he made a promise. He said "Mom, I promise never to do something without asking your permission again. I just wanted to surprise you with a warm car." That's Reuben. He was good to his promise too. He didn't do anything whatsoever without asking me for several months, even over a year. Then, about 18 months after he had driven my car into my rented house, he broke that promise.

# Chapter Two

## He Brought Faith Home

Reuben had a best friend named Jonathon. Reuben and Jon are still best friends to this day. When Reu came home in the 5th Grade he came home one day all excited because he had found himself a best friend. Not just a friend he told me, Jonathon was going to be his best friend and was going to play football with him. Reuben had been playing football for about a year and he wanted nothing more than to talk Jon into joining his team. Jon didn't like football all that much, but was actually more of a soccer fan. Over the years there would be many differences between the two best friends, but they have remained very close. When they were seventeen Jon called Reuben to tell him that his dog Princess had given birth to a lot of puppies. This was a big surprise to me, because I know I had actually given John's sister Janet money to have her dog Princess fixed so she couldn't have puppies. I knew Princess must have been twelve years old. That's very old for a dog to be having puppies. I was concerned not only for the puppies, but for Princess too.

Jon wasn't just calling Reu to say that Princess had puppies, he was calling to say that several of the puppies were born with problems and that they were either dead or dying, and that they needed to be buried and taken care of. He wanted Reu to go with him because that's what best friends do. I heard Reuben ask Jon if all of the dogs were dead—immediately I called out to him while he was on the phone. "No, Reuben, you cannot bring a dog home. You cannot bring a puppy home, do you hear me?" He heard me. He nodded his head and waved me off in a way that let me know that he had heard every word I said. Typically Reuben would do anything and everything I said. He wasn't a very rebellious kid, he actually made an effort to be a good son because he was the man of the house. He wanted to prove to me and to himself that he could make good decisions.

Remember the promise my son had made me after he drove the car through the kitchen wall? He was about to break that promise. He took off with Jonathon after kissing me on the head and saying "Don't worry Mom, I'm just burying the dead puppies and moving the lives ones to a warmer place." That was the last time I lived in a house with only one dog. We weren't even suppose to have the dog we had. The house belonged to our landlord Frank, who was very upset that we had Matrix. He had told me when I rented the house that I couldn't have a dog. Well, we didn't tell him about Matrix, because Matrix was staying with a friend at the time. I just knew that my son would keep his promise and that he would come home later that evening and work on his homework. He had a chapter of English to read and I was going to help him write the essay he was suppose to write.

Time ticked by and no sign of Reuben. I began washing dishes and just doing the last minute clean up before I was to sit down, read the daily newspaper, and go over my favorite section—the cartoons. One of the cartoons I always read is called Todd the Dinosaur. It's about a Dinosaur that is supposed to be in elementary school. He gets himself into all sorts of problems, and it's always cute. Todd is actually the creation of my good friend Patrick Roberts. Patrick and I go to the same church, and reading his cartoons about Todd makes me think of something he may have done when he was a kid growing up. In some cases Todd can be just like Reuben too. I bet

Todd hasn't brought home any puppies to his mother lately? Come to think of it, Todd doesn't have a mother.

The front door opened and in bounced my son. He was wearing his number 63 football jersey, and he was smiling. The jersey was tucked into his pants, which is something that he didn't usually do. He walked right into the kitchen and wouldn't stop smiling. I knew something was up. Reuben's belly was beginning to move a little bit. My eyes widened, and my mouth fell open. "Reuben! No! You didn't bring home a puppy. They can't be taken from their mom, they're only two weeks old." I protested, and I slammed down the dishtowel that had been over my shoulder. I was upset to the max because I had just told this boy he could not bring home a puppy, and there was no way that the thing under his jersey wasn't exactly that! I couldn't see it, but I could see the moving little bulge and I saw the big, fat, smile on his face. He immediately went into his defense mode, claiming that the dog was going to die if he hadn't saved it, it was going to be killed by its own mother. He described for me the way that Princess had been sitting on it . . . her, he said. It was a girl. Then, he began telling me how he couldn't let her die. He couldn't let Princess just sit on her head and suffocate her. He had to do something. He even tried to say that he only wanted to keep her until Princess let her come back, maybe when she was big enough to fight off the other dogs that wouldn't let her drink milk from her mom. Yeah, like that was going to happen.

I continued my protest. I was very straight-faced, I didn't give in. I wouldn't give in. I could not give into this. I was in charge, I was the mom. I was . . . . until he brought her out of his jersey, and she lay there without a single sound. She couldn't make a sound, even though she opened her mouth and I could see that she was trying to cry out. In an instant it was over. She looked up at me. She stared directly into my eyes with the face of a beaten angel. She had been hurt, she was just about to die, and all she could do was look up at me and ask without making a sound . . . if I would help. Reuben hadn't said another word. I couldn't stop staring at her face. I prayed and I asked God to make her live. I cried, and I took her from Reuben's hand. Her little left arm was bent back so far over her left shoulder that it looked like a broken Barbie doll's arm. He wanted to know if we could bend it back. No. It doesn't work that way I told him. Her right arm was completely gone and without the use of her left leg, I had no idea how she would ever learn to walk or get around in order to eat, go to the bathroom, or just be a normal dog.

# Chapter Three

Dr. Putnam

Faith lay in my hand for a little while, staring up into my face. I couldn't believe what I was about to do. I was about to give her a bath and let her stay in my house forever. Because she was so small and so young, barely a few weeks old, I didn't know if I could use dog shampoo on her in order to get the poo and hair mats out of her fur. I decided to use regular shampoo instead, and I held her very carefully in the sink to begin the washing process. It took several attempts. The poor puppy had been laying or rolling around in very nasty poo and dirt for days. I had no idea how long it had been since she had eaten, but she was beginning to nip and suck at the fingers to get the water from them into her belly. I hadn't thought about one of the things Reuben had said to me. He said she could go back perhaps after she was big enough to fight off the other dogs that were healthy in order to drink her mother's milk. How long had it been I wondered, was there something in the house I could use tonight?

When Reuben was a baby I didn't have the money to buy him regular baby formula and I found an old-fashioned formula in a recipe book. It called for Milnot, a brand name of canned milk, some corn syrup, vitamins that can be administered through an eye-dropper, and an equal share of distilled water. I argued with myself that dogs are not humans, but that if I left out the vitamins until I could talk to the doctor in the morning, I should be OK. I mixed the recipe and began giving Faith, or Little Yellow Dog, as she was called at that time, a bit of the mixture. She couldn't exactly suck it off my hand, but she could lick it somewhat, and her eyes completely changed from being scared and unsure to being overly anxious and full of excitement. Food!

I called the veterinarian's office and left a message on the answering service, as I knew that it was going to be after hours. Dr. Deana Putnam had an emergency number I could have called, and I almost did, but I wanted to be sure that the puppy would survive the night before I bothered her with an emergency to worry about. Dr. Putnam and I actually went to school together when we were kids. She was always a dog and cat lover, more cat than dog actually, but she wasn't the type of kid to go play hop-scotch or meet you at the swings. She was smarter, preferring to talk about the way things were made. It's no wonder she became a doctor of animals. With her extreme intelligence and love for animals she was destined to be one of the best vets I had ever met.

I called Dr. Putnam very early the next day. She suggested that I bring the puppy in. I did of course, and it didn't take long for her to show me why it would be very difficult for Faith to actually learn to walk. She had never in her professional years seen a dog without the use of both of its front legs. She had seen many three-legged dogs, dogs with a missing front or back limb, but never one that was missing both its front legs. Even though Faith had the little arm on her left side, it was most likely going to die, because it wasn't formed correctly. It didn't have an elbow, and it had seven toes on it. The arm was not going to be useful in terms of standing or putting weight on it. If Faith was to survive, according to the doctor, we had to get her off of her chest and up on her feet somehow. At the time, she was scooting a little and the doctor said that if she continued to scoot she would wear a hole in her chest, and possibly in her little chin, as she was using her chin to scoot across the floor. It had to hurt. I would watch her throw her tiny face down and pull it back quickly, forcing herself to scoot about an inch before she would throw her face down again. Dr. Putnam was right. We had to find a way to get her to sit up, maybe hop like a rabbit, and that would stop her from hurting her chin and from rubbing a hole in her chest. If she had rubbed a hole in her chest and chin she could have gotten an infection that would end up hurting her worse, and she could have died from the infection.

Dr. Putnam told me about Tiger's Milk, a formula for baby kittens that can be purchased over the counter. I used an eye-dropper and fed Faith this way for about two more weeks. It wasn't an easy thing to do. Because she would have naturally eaten every two hours or so from her mother, we had to set the alarm clock and get up every two hours and feed Faith. My daughters Laura and Caity were certainly up for the task. They fell in love with Faith immediately. Something that is not well known to the public about Faith, is that Reuben was her first owner. From the moment he brought her home until the day he moved out of the house in March of 2003, he was called Faith's owner. When he left he was going to give Faith to Caity, but she had recently talked me into getting yet another dog that supposedly was going to be Faith's best friend since our dog Matrix wasn't a puppy and wasn't interested in Faith whatsoever. When Caity told Reuben she wanted Laura to have Faith, Reuben agreed and that's how Faith became Laura's dog.

We set the alarm clock to ring in two-hour intervals. I got up first, and fed Faith, then I gave the clock to Laura, and she would get up in two hours. She passed it back to Caity, who then passed it back to Reuben. We literally worked around the clock to make sure Faith was trained to eat properly. Showing her how to use the bathroom outside was harder than we thought it was going to be, because we couldn't rub her nose in 'it' and expect her to go outside. We simply picked up the poo and carried it outside with us and with Faith, to show her where it was suppose to be deposited. Pee was a different story, and we knew it was going to be confusing. That's where her friend Ean comes in.

# Chapter Four

## Matrix and Ean

Matrix is a perfect dog. He is half Dachshund and half Beagle. He was found at a no-kill shelter called Pets and People in Yukon, Oklahoma. In fact, Dr. Putnam is one of the vets that Pets and People refers people to go see when they adopt a puppy. That's how I was reacquainted with my old friend. She was recommended to me through the shelter when I adopted Matrix. Matrix was adopted in 1999, when we were living in a rent house belonging to a woman who didn't care if we had pets. Soon after we adopted him he was trained by our cats to be the best cat ever. He wouldn't eat until he was told to. He wouldn't play until he was asked to. The cats had my poor puppy completely confused by the time he was six months old. We moved from the house when the lady sold it, and we were unable to keep our pets. This was perhaps one of the saddest moments of our lives because we had wanted so much to just live in a nice house and have our animals with us.

We allowed a nice family to adopt Matrix. It was snowing and we met them at a store between our house and their house. Several weeks later I received a phone call from the area Air Force Base. A Captain was calling me—telling me that he had found Matrix. I explained to him that he was no longer my dog. Perhaps the tag had not been updated. The family that adopted Matrix had set him free at the base in hopes that he would be found. He was found, and I agreed to allow the nice Captain to keep him. I did have to warn the good Captain that we had spoiled Matrix completely. He would have to sleep with the dog, and allow him to burrow under the covers. He would have to feed him several times a day, just a little bit, not a great deal all at once, and that he would have to go out only for a few minutes, as he was not an outdoor dog. I also mentioned to him that Matrix loved to sleep on the top of the couch when it wasn't night time. The Captain understood the rules, and welcomed my little fat dog into his life. We thanked God that Matrix was going to be taken care of.

Because of a divorce and several things that followed it, I was finally awarded full custody of my two girls on July 25, 2001. It was Caity's 11th birthday. Two days later I was allowed to take them with me forever, and all we wanted to do was to celebrate. I asked the girls what they wanted to do. Where they wanted to go. It would not have mattered to me if they had said they wanted to go to Disney World, I would have found a way. Thank goodness for me, they wanted to go to Pets and People so that they could play with dogs, bathe them, walk them, and clean up after the cats in the big cat room. My girls have always, perhaps like Dr. Putnam, been a bit more interested in animals than going to parks and shopping.

When we arrived at Pets and People, Laura was confronted with a big surprise. Matrix was dragging another volunteer who was trying to walk him, straight to Laura! It had been several months since I had given the Captain permission to keep Matrix. Seeing him at the shelter was simply unbelievable. He jumped up in the air, did a little dance, whined a great deal, and wiggled his way out of the leash that was holding him. He had found his people again. We took Matrix home with us forever. The really funny thing is, Matrix had been brought to Pets and People by the Captain when he had to go to Germany. Matrix had been adopted out three separate times over the past few months, and each time he had been brought back because he was simply too spoiled for any of the would-be new owners. We understood him, and we were so happy to have him back.

FLASH FORWARD to 2003, when we had just received notice from our landlord Frank that having Matrix in our new rental house was a violation. He charged us over $300 for having Matrix, and told us that if we violated the lease again he would ask us to leave. The day Reuben brought Faith home we had a cat as well as Matrix, but Frank didn't know it. After a few weeks of raising Faith with Matrix, trying to get the two of them to become friends, we decided it wasn't working for either Matrix or for Faith. She needed a friend her own age, someone to teach her how to go to the bathroom outside, and someone to teach her to stand up and hop, or play without scooting around the ground. Matrix, as perfect as he was, just wasn't interested in helping Faith to play.

It was very close to Valentine's Day when Caity saw an ad in the paper for a Welsh Corgi puppy. It wasn't as expensive as we thought it would be, and it wasn't too far away. We really weren't suppose to have dogs, but since we were already planning to move in the spring and we wanted to give Faith a buddy. We drove out to the country lot where a couple lived with their two Corgi dogs off the beaten path. It wasn't easy finding the lot in the fog, but we did find it, and when we arrived, the sound of so many yapping puppies came rolling out the front door to meet us. The only dog that didn't come out to greet us was a tri-color male puppy that hid himself under a couch. He tried to embed himself into the wallpaper, but was unable to do so when the hands of my daughter Caity reached for him and pulled him out to the living room rug. Ean. She had to have this puppy, and would not take another. He was named before she held him, a name she had borrowed from a popular television show where the hero dog, a red and white Corgi, is named Ean. It rhymes with fine.

Ean was shy at first, very shy. He didn't want to have anything to do with any of us. He was upset that we had taken him from his family. He was upset that we had taken him from his home.

He cried constantly, but wouldn't be consoled. He only wanted to be set free or perhaps taken back to his warm bed with his warm brothers and sisters to snuggle next to. When we brought Ean into the house he immediately ran under the chair in the front room and refused to come out for anyone. Faith was naturally curious about the new addition to the home, and she crawled under the chair to investigate. I wondered if Ean would become aggressive and bite her on the tip of her nose for trying to get a good look at him. To my surprise he stopped whining, and he stopped crying too. He wasn't shaking anymore and he wasn't backed up against the wall like he had been. He wanted to sniff Faith's yellow face as much as she wanted to sniff him.

It only took a few minutes for him to come out from the chair, and instantly the two of them were wrestling in the middle of the floor. Ean was snarling, barking, yapping, and carrying on, but Faith, because her voice box had been sat on, was unable to return the calls. She tried to. Her mouth opened, her jaw lowered, as she came after him again and again, but the only thing that managed to come forth from her mouth was a whiff of a sound really. Just a pip. I remember looking at Ean and thinking. "Maybe you can help her bark too."

Ean and Faith became inseparable. They fought and played all day long. It was during this time that we used several methods to get Faith up off the ground, trying to make her hop like a rabbit so that she could have a chance at survival. I'm going to jump a bit ahead of myself in the story, and tell you what happened on March 22, 2003, about five weeks after we brought Ean into the family.

We were training Faith to hop. She had managed to do it too. She had managed to get off the ground and to sit up like a rabbit or a squirrel. She still wasn't able to go fast, but she was moving and she was bounding across the room in giant hops that made all of us laugh nearly every time we saw it. Ean came into the room on one of these occasions. It was March 22, 2003, my son's 18th birthday. We were all outside playing with the dogs. I had just come from the grocery store and I had bones for all of the dogs to chew on. Big, meaty, bones—one for each. Suddenly, without warning, Ean came running straight at Faith. He had left his bone where he had dropped it, and he obviously decided to steal her bone to add to his. He was quick and stealth in his attack. Corgis are categorized through the kennel clubs as herding dogs. Most Corgis go on to become good sheep or cattle dogs, whereas Ean became a pet and was Faith's constant companion. Whether natural instinct kicked in, or he was just feeling good about the first week of spring having arrived, we don't know, but he ran straight at Faith full force. He knocked her from her sitting position, bit her on the ankle, and stole her bone right out of her mouth. Running away with it he was almost smiling. He wasn't looking back to see her reaction, perhaps he truly believed he had gotten away with it. Not so! Faith, determined not to lose her bone to anyone, literally hopped up from a laying position. She landed on her feet, and putting one foot in front of the other, began running! She quickly gained her speed and was upon the dog faster than anything I can remember having witnessed. She stood completely up on the pads of her feet, towering over Ean like a Tyrannosaurus Rex! She grabbed the back of Ean's furry neck and thrashed him around in the air like a rag doll. She then retrieved her bone and walked back to where she had been . . . like nothing spectacular had just happened.

Our dog could run! This was a miracle. We knew at that moment that naming her Faith was the right thing to do. We stopped calling her all of the other little names we were used to calling her, Little Yellow Dog, Puppy, Yellow Mutt, and so forth. We just called her Faith. Caity joked that she should be called Terror. Ean no doubt agreed with Caity. He wasn't sure if he had been allowed to live or if Faith was more interested in her bone. He stayed away from her for a little while, only venturing to watch her from the other side of the yard that day. The evening fell and with it came forgiveness. Faith didn't share her bone with Ean, but she did share her blanket. Pulling it off the couch with her teeth, she laid on it and made a little barking-yappy sound. The first one we had ever heard her make. The sound was directed at Ean. He came over and they began licking each other's snouts. They were friends again.

As time went on Ean developed a skin disorder that Dr. Putnam said was very odd, not quite rare, but difficult and expensive to treat. We tried keeping up with it for a while, but it wasn't easy to continue paying for medicine for the dog when I wasn't working full time and needed the money to feed my kids. We found a Corgi Rescue group in Oklahoma, and allowed them to adopt Ean, who we called Corgus at times. We are told that he made a full recovery, but that he would be on medication all of his life to keep the hair on his back from falling out, and that the disease was not passed on to his offspring. He is currently living on a farm where again, we are told, that he has made lots of little tri-color and red and white baby Corgis. I'm sure they are quite beautiful.

# Chapter Five

Let it Snow, Let it Snow!

There is a famous picture of Faith when she is about six weeks old. She is standing in the snow, and if you look around her, you will see that the snow is completely uninterrupted. There are no paw prints or drag marks around the edges of the snow where she is sitting. That is because the day we decided to force her to stand up on her own, we went out into the backyard, (all of us, we are all guilty) and we placed her in the snow butt first. Yes, we took our camera with us because we had a feeling that the feisty little dog we had loved for almost a month, was going to do something that would be camera worthy. We were right. She stared up at us at first, perhaps wondering why we were leaving her in the cold, wet, snow. She couldn't take it much longer than twenty or thirty seconds, and she used her back leg muscles to hoist herself into the air into a full standing position. SNAP! We got the picture!

In the picture you will notice that her left arm looks as if it is not attached to her body. It was so far back behind her, literally on her shoulder. Later, as time went on her left arm sort of 'fell' into a flopping position beside her shoulder, not quite the normal looking position for an arm, but it was no longer placed behind her. We also noticed at that time that she was using the arm as a guide, a balance—when she rounded corners, she seemed to throw it out first. In the snow that late afternoon, Faith stood up on her very own. She wanted us to pick her up, she wanted us to dry off her wet bum. We refused. I know we were laughing, but we were trying not to. We were trying to be firm and strong for her; it wasn't easy. The snow outside had been sent for her I believe. She had been perfectly content to stay on the ground until this moment. We didn't pick her up, in fact, we continued to play with Matrix (we didn't have Ean at this point) and we made sure she realized we were having fun with Matrix, running around, throwing snow, making snow angels, and basically not including Faith.

She wanted to play, she wanted to have fun, but she didn't know what to do in order to get to us. That's when it happened. She must have thought about it, she must have said to herself "They're over there, and I'm over here", because she decided on her own to take that first big hop. It was only one hop. As soon as she did it we were all so overwhelmed that we left poor Matrix frolicking alone and we all ran to the puppy. She was immediately snatched up by one of the girls, and we made the biggest fuss over her. We gave her gummi bears, hugs, kisses, we told her how great she was, and we began playing with her in the snow. Matrix turned and walked back into the house. It was sad. I went back in and loved on him, leaving the girls to play with Faith. This would be just one of the thousands of times that Matrix has had to endure more humility than any dog should be required to do. He makes the sacrifice because he obviously realizes that he was born with four working legs, and that she is the one that needed our help. Today Matrix is more than used to being forgotten by the public, even by the girls from time to time, but I will never let him forget that I love him. He is MY dog. In fact, I dedicated this book to him for his kind-hearted generosity toward Faith. I tell him, "Matrix, you are perfect in every way".

It snowed several more times in 2003, deep, fluffy snow that allowed us to put Faith in the white frothy stuff over and over again. We drug her around on skateboards in the snow to show her what it was like to run in the snow. We put her in a wagon but she hopped out, and we were afraid she would hurt herself, so we ditched the wagon and put her back on the skateboard again. We used a sock and because she is half Chow, she would grab the end of the sock and refuse to let go. We used this flaw in her character to literally pick her up by her jaws and drag her through the snow until she began hopping in it to keep up with us. We weren't being mean. We never went really fast, and we never would have picked her up by her neck, but her jaws are very strong, like those of a Pit Bull—Chows are perhaps the Chinese equivalent to the American Pit Bull in terms of having really strong jaw pressure. She will grab onto a sock today and I can still pick her straight off the ground without fear that she's going to let go and fall. She won't let go. It's part of their nature. The dog I had when I was a teenager was half Chow and I learned then how not to allow her to grab onto my arm when we were playing. Ouch! My hand still has a scar where Chrissy, tried to take back her toy from me. She dug her pointed teeth so deeply into my hand that her teeth touched! She and I both were equally upset about it, but I was the one with the hole in my hand.

Faith loves the snow. When it snows now she loves to run in it, slide on her face and chest and make her rendition of a snow angel. We were filming the Maury Show in New York City in the winter of 2004, when they asked us to do a family home video. They took us to a nice house in New Jersey, and it could have been our house I guess, but it was two stories, beautiful, and way out of our price range. We loved it. Faith ran around the front yard sliding, and gliding through the snow. The cameraman picked up so much of the fun, and kept the part where she was catching snow balls and eating them. We had to remind her not to eat yellow snow, and we wouldn't let the cameraman film her making yellow snow either! Faith barks like crazy now. She doesn't let anything stop her from doing whatever it is that she wants to do . . . playing in the snow is one of her favorite things to do, and because it makes my dog happy, I say "God, let it snow! Let it snow! Let it snow!"

# Chapter Six

## Getting Her Move On

When Reuben brought Faith home to me I was working part time at a college called Oklahoma City Community College. He brought her home to me on January 21, 2003, just after the Spring Semester had already started at most colleges around the country. I had previously, just the semester before, worked for three colleges. Due to budget cuts I was released, and was thinking about taking the certification tests to become a middle school or high school teacher. I needed to work. I knew that it would be an entire semester before I could be hired because teachers are not usually hired in the middle of the school year, not unless there is a surprise opening.

The fact that I wasn't working full time meant that I could give more time to Faith in training her how to walk upright, and to hop so that she could get her move on. We really couldn't afford to let her scoot across the floor and possibly hurting herself. Not to mention that it just didn't suit her personality. She didn't seem like the type of animal that would want to be seen laying on the floor or being unable to stand up to the world. She was a fighter. We knew this. I decided to take a part time job typing for attorneys in the area and simply working from home as well as teaching the two classes I was assigned to teach at Oklahoma City Community College.

The college also played an unexpected role in getting Faith up on her back legs, and they weren't even meaning to be a part of that history. I worked in the Arts and Humanities Department of the college. The Arts and Humanities Department handled subjects such as English, Ceramics, Music, Philosophy, and of course, Art, courses in drawing, painting, and computer design. I was an English Instructor, and my hours were from 5:30 p.m. to 10:30 p.m. one night a week. This left plenty of time to work during the day typing, and plenty of time to go about begging people to help me to design some sort of mechanism that my dog could use to get up off the ground.

I took little Faith to the college when she was about 4 or 5 weeks old. She was the talk of the Security Office because upon arriving she immediately left a little brown deposit on their floor. Every officer in the office had to giggle a little, but no one was jumping to clean it up. I remember asking any of them if they wanted to frame it because she was indeed the only two-legged dog any of them had ever laid eyes on. We decided to throw the present away. Faith was cuddled and snuggled by everyone in the Security Office, and we registered her as an official guest because she was about to visit the Mechanic Engineering students to see, if anything, they could do for her.

Sadly, their professor who handled actual designing of carts and tools was going to be out for quite a bit of the semester. The curriculum was set for the students to begin working with, and the assignments could simply not be changed. Without realizing what she was telling me, one of the administrators of the department suggested that I come back next semester before the curriculum could be locked in. Perhaps then something could be done. I looked at her. I looked long and hard, and I thought about laughing, but it wasn't a laughing matter. I told her "Faith is 5 weeks old now. In fall she will be more than 8 months old. She will already be able to walk at that point, and we won't need a cart to train her." There was nothing they could do . . . or, nothing they were willing to do. One or two students in the college who were also my students suggested that they independently come up with some sort of a plan to help, but it actually never happened. I don't know why. I then made a couple of phone calls and sent out a couple of e-mails to places I found on Google when I simply put in the keywords "dogs with disabilities". The two websites that came up were: *www.wheelchairsfordogs. com* and *www.dogswithdisabilities.com*. After long and exhausting explanations on the phone with the owners and/or managers of both sites, it was apparent that neither site had been prepared to work with dogs without front legs. I was literally going to be on my own. At least I had my innovative and exploring children to help me.

Faith may not have realized it, but what we were doing with her was actually rehabilitating her. We were literally training her to do something that isn't suppose to be done, but that could be done if trained. We had to teach her how to use muscle groups that are not ordinarily used for propping up dogs, or to allow them to be in a standing or upright sitting position. From time to time my dog Matrix, because he is part Dachshund, will sit up and beg like you see Dachshunds do—balancing on their butts. He will do that for a few seconds and then lower his body back to a normal walking stance. If we could get Faith to sit up like that, and to remain seated, she could at least be off the ground. That was one goal. The other goal was to get her to propel herself in a forward motion that would resemble a rabbit hopping. Frogs do it, but they put their legs behind themselves. Rabbits use the foot itself to push from, using every long muscle in the leg. Rabbits have very long legs. Faith's legs didn't look that long. We had to give it a try.

Using what we knew would be interesting to her, peanut butter on a spoon, we led her around the house with the sock in her mouth trick. She couldn't put her head down or we wouldn't give her any peanut butter. After a few trips around the living room, Faith understood that her head had to be lifted up, the peanut butter was WAY up in the air, not near the ground. If she wanted any of that good, gooey, sticky peanut butter, she had to look up. Every time she began looking up and trying to move without using her chin we would reward her. While we were dragging her around with the sock, if she got up onto her back legs and hopped after us, we gave her peanut butter and we gave her a gummi bear. We had no idea how long she was willing to be subjected to this therapy. We just kept working with her for weeks and weeks.

One day Laura put a spoonful of peanut butter on a paper plate and laid the paper plate on top of my bed. The bedroom door was left open, and of course little curious Faith had to edge herself into the room. She was there when I came in from the grocery store. She was whining and starting to make gurgling sounds, but nothing like a bark. She couldn't see the peanut butter but her nose was working overtime. It was moving, and it was twitching faster than fast. I put a couple of pillows on the floor and sat her on top of one to let her be even closer. Yes, this was torture, I understand, but we did have to make her do something for herself. She did something that evening that surprised everyone. She must have somehow invited Ean to climb onto the pillow with her. Then, using Ean as a dog-step ladder, she literally climbed on top of him and it was just enough for her to reach the bed. Using her teeth to pull herself up onto the covers, she found the prize! Not that she shared a single lick with her frolicking friend just below her who was still just shy of being big enough to jump on the bed by himself. No, she was there alone, on the top of the world—licking the spoon! The winner! We've always said that Faith is a bit smarter than the average dog, this proved it. (Of course, we had to reward our Little Eanster. He was given more love than ever, and a full spoon of peanut butter as well.)

That determination that Faith showed us in her attempt to get the peanut butter off the spoon that had been placed on top of the bed is called something. Not only would we humans say that it was persistence, we would call it doggedness! I have seen several more instances with Faith where her dogged determination would not let her be less of a dog. She and I were walking in the Dolese Park in the spring of 2003. She couldn't have been more than four months old. We were waiting on Reuben to finish some sort of a sporting event across the street at his high school Putnam City High School. We were just walking alone the edge of the playground when suddenly a squirrel came running out of the barrel on the "big toy". It stopped for a split second when it saw Faith, probably not sure of what to make of a two-legged dog. This was after she had learned to walk upright, and he was simply confused. Without notice Faith bound toward the squirrel and chased him over 100 yards through woods, trees, over a low-hanging wire, (hopped it) and just kept going until the squirrel finally decided that a tree would be the best place for him to get away. Up he ran, and if she could have Faith would have flown up into the tree right along after the fuzzy creature. She hopped straight up several times trying to reach him, but alas, he had escaped. I had to run hard to catch her, and believe me, I had a fun time explaining to the children who watched her that she wasn't an ordinary dog. Breathless by the time I pulled her back, I latched her leash back to her and we walked back to the car so I could cross the main street to pick my son up. I was so proud of Faith. I told her that she was just as normal as any other dog I had ever met—or had to chase down. She wanted that squirrel.

# Chapter Seven

## Channel 4—KFOR-TV

By now everyone has heard of Faith the Two-Legged Dog. She's even a trademark. It didn't happen immediately, but it did actually happen overnight. On a bright sunny afternoon in June of 2003, we were playing in the backyard of our house with the dogs and I was thinking about the world's problems while the kids were running around trying to play keep away with Ean and Faith. There was a war going on in Iraq, shortage of oil, dry hot weather in states that needed rain for the wheat to grow, and wildfires in several states including Oklahoma. The news was literally filled with bad news and very little good or happy news. I knew it wasn't much to offer, but I thought I would call a local station and see if I could interest them in doing a little feel-good story about a dog that had managed to stand up on her own two legs, balance, and walk. In fact, by June of 2003, Faith was running, skipping, hopping, even dancing when she felt like it. I just thought the city of Oklahoma City and its surrounding neighboring communities could use a little happy news.

Linda Cavanaugh is a beautiful anchor at station KFOR-TV Channel 4 in Oklahoma City. It was Linda that I called to see about doing a little story on Faith. At first her producers were hesitant, saying that they weren't sure it was something they would be interested in, but they know Linda and they know she would love to do a story of a dog that had adapted to walking upright—overcoming obstacles. Little did anyone realize at KFOR-TV that the story cameraman Dan Alexander was about to shoot was extraordinary. Upon arriving to our house Dan began unloading his camera and his tripod. It wasn't a big set of equipment, and he didn't have any lighting rigs with him. We were going to be shooting outside, maybe a run around the neighborhood. I had explained to the producer on the telephone that Faith walked upright, but for some reason the message had not been fully understood. The producer had told Dan that the dog walked a little on its back feet, probably a few feet and was a happy little dog. To Dan's utter amazement, Faith ran up to him, 37" tall and moving one foot in front of the other all the way from the front door to his truck. He nearly fell over!

Grabbing his camera and tripod in one hand he quickly made a telephone call on his cell with the other. He explained to the person he had reached that the dog walked upright on its (her) feet—like a human! It was the first time anyone had actually used the term. Like a human! Yes, that's exactly how Faith walks. Now, from time to time she hops, skips, and jumps, but when she walks she appears to be a bit bow-legged, understandably because of her leg structure, but yes, she walks like you and I do. Dan began giving us instructions to go across the yard, then back again, can she go up stairs, can she hop over the curb, can she run around the neighborhood a bit? He followed Faith and questioned us for the boom microphone. I think I answered one or two questions but because Faith was truly Laura's dog, Laura did a full interview with Dan and mentioned something that most news stations would not have allowed. She gave the credit for Faith being able to walk to God. When the sound bite came through over the air, and God was credited for Faith's ability to amaze everyone, we couldn't have been more proud of both Faith and of Laura for thinking of it. We were also extremely proud and grateful to KFOR-TV for airing it.

That night, June 23, 2003, Linda Cavanaugh, close to breaking a tear in her eye while delivering the story, told the citizens of the state of Oklahoma about an unusual dog. "Sometimes these stories leave you scratching your head in wonder" she said. She went on to show the video, and to explain that Faith was like any other dog, chasing our cats around the house. Later that night I received a phone call. Seems the news room was flooded with calls about Faith. Linda wanted to put the story on the AP, the Associated Press, and it would go out to the entire world if that happened. I said yes. By the next morning I was on the phone talking with representatives from not only news stations, but magazines, television shows, people who were curious about my dog Faith. From just before 4:00 a.m. to past 11:00 a.m. the next day I was talking on the phone to both domestic and international media reporters. I was not surprised to see that on Keith Olbermann's MSNBC show *Countdown*, that Faith was the number one story of the day. Wow! All because she wanted to do something the every other dog did—walk.

# Chapter Eight

## Ripley's Believe it or Not

Laura and I decided to go to the KFOR-TV station a couple of days later to actually introduce Faith to the rest of the crew at the station. While we were there a phone call came in for us. That was in itself unbelievable but it was true. The really funny part was that the phone call was from Ripley's Believe it or Not. Who is going to believe that Ripley's called me at the news station when I don't ever go to the station? It happened. They must have been calling the station because Linda Cavanaugh put the story on the AP, but since we were there visiting I took the call. Ripley's had seen the coverage of Faith on the AP and wanted to do a story about her. The next Saturday Ripley's sent a lady named Jeannie to our house. She showed up with a film crew from Dallas. It was their job to film Faith in various settings so that the world could see exactly what kind of dog Faith is.

Here's the crazy part. They wanted to do a day-in-the-life type show about Faith, which if it was truly a day-in-the-life of Faith would be filmed from under the bed all day because in reality that's where Faith is most of the time. They didn't want that. They wanted to do a show where Faith was at the ball park, the duck pond, a restaurant, walking down busy streets downtown where she could see people, make friends, and be a huge inspiration to all mankind. OK—but she never does that, or at least she hadn't before they shot their footage. Today things might be a bit different. We do travel around the country with Faith, and we do go to shops, stores, hospitals, military bases, and do shows for people who invite us. In early July 2003, Faith was happy to lay under the bed all day and think about chewing up an old sock. This would not have been a good episode for Ripley's (believe it or not).

Jeannie and her crew had staged a breakfast scene in our house where the entire family was to sit down at the beginning of the busy Saturday and just eat together. How many of us do that? We don't, but it was fun to pretend. Reuben and Caity, not waiting for the rest of us, decided to eat the real food before we were finished filming the over-extended schedule outside. By the time Laura and I came to the table (we had even allowed a friend to be there to make it look like we had friends over for breakfast), all of the real food was gone! Faith looked fatter too, so I think Reuben and Caity were sharing their spoils with her and probably with Matrix and Ean as well.

Jeannie had the crew go out and get bread from a local bakery so we could at least appear to be sharing a good breakfast. She then staged my parents to walk through the door on this busy, hustling Saturday that we were all gathered at the table. Yes, my parents were well dressed, mom wearing her make up, and dad coming in with a big grin on his face. The problem with this scene was that my dad, bless his heart, was too thin for the show's audience. Jeannie told her crew, not me, to drop the shot of my dad because she didn't need e-mails and telephone calls about the skinny man coming through the door. I wasn't told until later by one of the camera crew, and before the show aired I remember telling my dad that he should gain weight if he was to be a big splash in Hollywood. He just laughed.

To say that Ripley's staged every scene would be very true. Nothing that was shot that day had been natural, but it worked. We went to a ball game in the park and let dozens of kids pet Faith. We went downtown and saw hundreds of excited people who had never seen Faith. They rushed in and out of restaurants and shops on the city's new canal walk way to see a two-legged dog walking upright like a human. Finally, in the last shot of the day something natural happened. A boy with his mother came walking up the pier, naturally. He was a blind boy, and his mother was leading him by the arm. He could hear noises and knew that something was going on in front of him. Almost without thinking I picked Faith up and walked her over to the mother and boy, asking the mother if she would allow her son to pet Faith. The family began to gather around them, there were several siblings that had been walking in front of the boy and his mother. All of them surrounded the boy and laughed and spoke in Spanish to him about the dog and that there was a camera crew. I tried to tell them that it was Ripley's Believe it or Not. I think Jeannie spoke to them in their language and explained that she would need them to sign a release. The boy was overjoyed, I was crying because this is what I believe Faith is good at doing. She is more of a people-dog, not a show-off.

Ripley's ran their segment of Faith in October, and millions of people watched as a little two-legged yellow dog made her way through neighborhoods, parks, downtown streets, and finally to a little blind boy with the biggest of smiles. The host explained very well how Faith was able to walk upright, how she was trained, and how much her family truly loved her. Even if her family doesn't sit down to the table on a Saturday morning with eggs, bacon, rolls, juice, milk, and coffee . . . we do love our Faith. The show has been replayed so many times in syndication. It has been three years and I am still hearing people tell that they have seen her on a re-run. Faith even appeared in a Ripley's Believe it or Not book. Her story is very small, not very long, but to be named at all is a great honor if you ask me.

# Chapter Nine

## PBS-TV the Rest of the World

After Ripley's came by to do a show about Faith several other shows wanted to do them as well. Some of the camera crews that came by filmed before Ripley's aired but we had signed a contract with Ripley's saying that we would allow them to be the first to tell the story internationally. Almost immediately following the KFOR-TV coverage I got a call from the famous, or infamous, depending on how you look at it, National Enquirer. They wanted to run a little story about Faith too. I had to think about that one. I didn't want to go to the grocery store and see Batboy screaming at my dog, or see a headline about Faith being from another planet.

I was happy and surprised to find out that the National Inquirer, the Star, the Globe, all of the store tabloids actually write true stories too. This is good because Faith's story has shown up in at least three weekly type tabloids including the National Enquirer, which was the first to run her story in this forum. The man who interviewed me over the telephone told me that he had seen the story on the AP and wanted to know everything. He was most interested in the way we trained Faith to walk upright, and what methods we used to physically motivate her. When I told him that peanut butter and gummi bears were used he laughed and said that he puts gummi bears on his peanut butter sandwiches, so he completely understood. What a great idea! I went straight to the store and bought a bag of gummi bears that morning. For lunch I put gummi bears on all of our sandwiches and today it's hard to imagine a peanut butter sandwich without the shiny, wiggly, jelly bears staring up at me just before I squish them into the bread and peanut butter. Faith thinks she's died and gone to Heaven when she rounds the corner of the kitchen on the days I make gummi bear/peanut butter sandwiches for lunch. She's always first in line.

The Oklahoma Public Television station out of Tulsa was not going to be left behind in all of the coverage that was taking place. They wanted their story too. It was filmed before the Ripley's show aired, but again because of our contract with Ripley's we made them wait just a day or two before showing their footage of a day-in-the-life of Faith. It was much the same as Ripley's had been but they did do something I found a bit more interesting and entertaining. They were able to put pictures of Faith on their show when she was a puppy and make the still pictures look as if they were moving. They had snow falling and everything. That was cool. Faith did something funny that I have rarely told anyone during the filming for the Tulsa Times show. The producer Royal Ailes had come to our house and was really impressed with Faith's abilities to walk and to catch things that were being thrown to him. He decided to toss a ball at her and play a little fetch. Well, no one obviously mentioned to Mr. Ailes that Faith is not the type of dog to fetch. No, she's a bit of a diva as a matter of fact. When Royal threw the ball it went straight into the air above Faith's head. She obliged him by watching the ball, and she followed it's landing with her eyes. She then looked at him with her head slightly cocked to the side, as if asking him if he was going to pick it up and entertain her again with his abilities to throw balls into the air.

Faith has always been a bit of a comedian. We aren't sure if she is doing this on purpose, or if she truly is too spoiled to get the bigger picture as to what dogs normally do when things are thrown at them. For Faith, a ball in the air is a demonstration, a thing to enjoy—much like a butterfly flitting around. A quickly-hurled stick across the yard to Faith looks more like a way for the person who threw it to find themselves running back and forth in front of her. She gets excited yes, but not because she has any intention of getting the stick, she wants to run back and forth with the person who is throwing it hoping to engage her in a game. We learned this early on and simply haven't told many people because quite honestly it is fun to watch their faces when the dog stares at them, egging them on to do it again, and again, and again.

The Tulsa Times airing was more information and less entertaining. We felt that it better told Faith's unique tale, and we encouraged many other stations to pick it up. After PBS stations in our own state came several film crews from across the world. Literally, people from Switzerland, Germany, Korea, and England were flying overseas to do a segment for their countries, stories again that would show the every day life of an extraordinary dog. Try as I might, I couldn't convince any of these stations to simply put their cameras on the ground facing the underneath of my bed—which I promised to have cleaned out, so that they could capture the true life story of the most amazing dog ever to live. Each and every crew wanted something that no one had filmed before. I kept offering, but no one took me up on it. So, we were off to the races—the horse races. It was fun to see the German crew running around setting up their equipment to capture the ponies running around the arena, and seeing Faith outside the stands as if that was a natural occurrence, it wasn't of course, but they told me that people in Germany would love it. We took them to a park to see ducks and geese being chased into the water, and for the first time ever Faith was filmed swimming. It wasn't pretty and I'm sure they decided to edit it from their film. It more or less appeared that we were allowing our dog to drown on public television. She didn't drown of course, but when she puts her head completely underwater and drives her body forward like Ariel in the Little Mermaid, one has to wonder if she's having fun or merely trying to survive the event. She was still wagging that spotted tongue of hers, so we had to keep the momentum going.

Off to the dog park with the Swiss. They were more interested in what other dogs thought of her. They wanted to film her at a school, but we couldn't get one in the summer. It was June of 2004 when they arrived. We settled for a Vacation Bible School, but interestingly my own church declined to let us film. That was heartbreaking for me because I was used to bringing Faith into the church for services and Sunday School on a near-weekly basis. To be denied a visit on camera for legal reasons was sad, but nevertheless understood. We found an inner city church that had no problems whatsoever with filming Faith and their kids. We danced with them, made balloon shapes, and even held races to see if any of them could out run Faith. To this day I have never seen the footage, but I do hope the people in Switzerland have seen it and have fallen in love.

The Koreans were hilarious! First, they hired a girl from a local college to interpret for them because I don't speak any other language other than English. The director and his crew were native to Korea and spoke very little English. They actually understood what I was saying, but they couldn't relate back to me quickly what it was that they wanted to do. We drove to a near by farm to show the Oklahoma countryside to their audience because again, no other film crew had filmed in the country. At that time Laura had a horse named Gracie and she kept her at a local farm. We drove to the farm where we were greeted very happily by three blond children that lived next door. Seth, Shiloh, and Lily. To put it bluntly, Lily is perhaps the most beautiful little girl in the entire world. Immediately, when you see her you remember the absolutely gorgeous smile of JonBenet. White blond hair literally flowing behind her, Lily was about four at the time we shot at the farm. She walked straight up to the cameraman to say hello, and I know he was amazed at her beauty because he shot footage of her constantly. As she played in the trees, bushes, around the haystacks, over the bridge, through the pond, and into the trails that lead off from the farm he continued to shoot. The animals on the farm were very much into their roles. Horses ran up and down the fence line trying to get a better look at Faith as she walked upright toward them. Shiloh had a pet peacock that he ran to get and when he saw Faith he opened up his gorgeous tail and thrashed his brilliant colors as strongly as he could to shoo her away from his hen that he felt Faith was getting a little too close to. Interestingly, the Korean crew found some of the strangest things to be fun and camera worthy. They shot footage of cow dung, and of one of their men stepping into the cow dung. There's plenty on a farm to see—and we decided to show them something they would never forget.

Now, I don't want you to think that we're too deeply rooted into the country, or that we find strange behavior in teenagers to be something of a common occurrence. We don't, but Laura, Seth and Shiloh couldn't resist themselves when they saw the camera crew filming the cow poop. They began picking up horse poop and throwing it at each other. Screaming, throwing, hitting each other with the messy stuff and yes, hitting Faith. Faith, being the complete diva that she is, retreated far, far away under a truck immediately. The cameraman didn't know which way to shoot. He was laughing so hard he told the interpreter to make the kids do it slower so he could really get a better angle. The kids had no problems going into a really slow-motion effect for the show. Give them an inch and they will stretch it out to the full mile. Slowing down to a snail's crawl the three of them pretended to be in a fierce battle using manure as ammunition. Dying was something really to be seen . . . dramatic, long-lasting, and with the flare of many rocket candles. Faith, for her part, crawled even further under the cab of the old truck—completely out of poo's-way. Lily sat on the fence giggling at her brothers, but hoping Laura would win.

When we broke for lunch the entire crew wondered if they would be allowed into the restaurant with dirt and other natural materials on their shoes. After a quick dusting off, and a complete change of wardrobe for Laura, we said good bye to our good friends on the farm and headed for the Lone Star Restaurant where for the first time in their lives these men had American Bar B-Q. If only the cameras could have been rolling at that meeting. Faith of course, was allowed in the restaurant. She has a bright orange vest that she wears for such occasions. If we had the sense to roll the cameras, the people of Korea would have been able to witness my little dog stealing a BBQ rib from one of the producers. With lightening speed over the top of the table, Faith was able to snag that rib. Oh, the benefits of being famous, no one ever gets onto Faith for being Faith, in fact, usually they apologize to her for not having offered their food to her in the first place. Will they ever learn? Faith, before she is anything else, is a dog.

# Chapter Ten

New York City!

Faith had never before flown on an airplane, and for that matter, neither had Laura. We were invited to New York City to be on the Ricki Lake Show, a show that is no longer on the air, but in the fall of 2003 was very popular and very fun to be a part of. We knew that Ricki Lake loved animals and that she had children, so we were glad when she said that she would be bringing her son Owen to the set so that he could see Faith too. I think he was just over two years old. Before we arrived in New York City we had to get past security in the Oklahoma City airport. That was a blast! Faith has never flown in the belly of the plane, but always up in the cabin with us. We would not fly to a show if they asked us to put Faith in cargo. She isn't cargo, Faith is a celebrity. We have never demanded to sit in First Class, but rather in the bulkhead, which is located just behind First Class so that Faith can lay down on the floor and be as comfortable as she can be.

Ricki's people made it possible for Laura and I to fly with Faith through Chicago. It had been a while since I had flown as well, and to be honest I was a little queasy on the first leg of the trip. A very nice lady in Chicago caught up with me because she wanted to see my dog—the same dog she and her kids had seen on Ripley's just a few days before on a rerun. She could tell that I wasn't walking exactly straight forward and offered to help me. She was a pharmaceutical representative with Wyeth products and she offered to give me a compound mix that helped with dizziness and nausea on the plane. Turns out she may actually be a cousin of mine. We sat down on the plane and departed for Newark where she went her way and I went mine. We had truly enjoyed our conversation. I couldn't have been more surprised than I was a couple of days later to find her standing again in the airport, at my gate, on my flight, and this time we were headed for St. Louis on our way home. She was flying through St. Louis on her way home to Arkansas. They say it's a small world, but sometimes it can really be shocking. Kim, the representative from Wyeth, called her husband and kids to tell them that she once again was flying with us, and again we were able to arrange it so that she sat with us on the plane as well. We sang Bee Gee songs and laughed about getting older, but Faith was just happy to hear us laughing. Flying kind of gets to her too. She found herself crawling onto Kim's lap and letting her hold on to her yellow body for most of the flight. Kim didn't even mind the occasional licking of the face, which usually occurs with Faith in flight. Some people may have been offended by such open affection.

Faith's appearance on Ripley's had actually flowered into something bigger. Her segment was considered one of the best ever shows on Ripley's, and this was the premise for the Ricki Lake Show. She did an annual Best of Ripley's Show. We were to appear on the stage with several incredible acts such as a man that had transformed himself with tattoos, plastic surgery, and dental work to look like a tiger. His name is Dennis Smith, and he is really a very interesting person. Faith wasn't sure what to think of him when she saw him walking down the hallway of greenrooms and toward our room, but she was very polite and licked his clawed "paw" nevertheless. He smiled, showing all of his pointed teeth, and rubbed her on the head. A tattooed man was on the show that day. There was a man that looked so much like Michael Jackson that people wanted to hire him for television and movies, and there was a guy who—if you want to believe it—would suck milk or other liquids up and through his nose using a long tube. No, I'm not lying, it is true, and we were there to see it all happening right in front of our eyes. Ricki was so happy to see Faith. She asked me several questions and then asked Laura a lot of questions about Faith. Due to the time limits on the show, only the questions that she asked Laura were aired. One of the funny things that happened on stage, and it was aired, is that Faith stood up when she was ready to leave the stage, and she simply walked into the audience, she was ready to go. Ricki just laughed and clapped her hands. The audience followed; when Faith has had enough she has no problem letting you know it.

New York City awaited us. We had a driver named Tony who could not have been a better stereotypical demonstration of what a real live New York Chauffeur was suppose to be. First, we were driven around in a huge, black, sleek, Suburban. The type with the tinted windows, and it even had a flag on the front, making it look as if we were from another country or something. We were important people with important things to do. Today we were going to the park. Central Park. From the studio where Ricki Lake filmed to the park wasn't very far, so we arrived at the south entrance to the park within a few minutes. Before we arrived however, Tony completed three telephone conversations with business associates, cussing at them, calling them idiots, and working his point of view into the conversation. At one point he took his hands off the steering wheel and used them to gesture at the phone. Tony was of Italian descent, and it was probably very normal for him to speak using his hands, but our eyes widened as he drove through bustling New York City traffic at high speeds without his hands on the wheel. I wasn't about to say anything to him. Tony was a big as a barn and had the smile of a shark! I loved him.

When we arrived at the park he informed us that he wasn't suppose to be driving us to see the sights, but that he had some business in the park. He would be about thirty minutes, so we should enjoy ourselves. Oh, that was all it took. We were out of the truck as fast as we could be, walking in the brisk City air, running through the most famous park in the world, looking for horse-pulled carriages, vendors, people playing basketball, all the things you see going on in Central Park. I don't think we would have been that upset if we had seen Tony shaking someone down. We were in our little fantasy world, talking out what was running through our heads at the time. Laura turned to me and smiled broadly when she saw Tony walking up to a group of guys all wearing long leather coats, except Tony; his leather jacket was tight, and short to the waist. He wore a black leather beret too, and had the blunt-toed boots you see body-guards wearing. What could they be doing?

Suddenly both Laura and I realized that we had been watching Tony, but we hadn't been paying the much attention to Faith. She was on her leash of course, but I thought Laura had her and she thought I had her. None of us had Faith! I didn't know which direction we had come from, having never been in the park before. Laura remembered a gold statue, but now we saw two. Faith! Where could she be? She would obviously have been seen by someone, and it didn't take long before we heard the laughing, saw the people pointing, and then we realized that Faith had simply had enough of sitting by our feet. She had stood up, walked off and probably chased a squirrel or something and then didn't know which way she had run. Both Laura and I saw her at the same time. Tony's little business group were among those laughing the hardest. So that no one worries too much about Faith, the park was brightly lit, it was in the early afternoon when hundreds of people are in the park walking their dogs correctly, and Faith being Faith would never have allowed anyone to take her home with them. She shies away from strangers when they attempt to pick her up. By this time in her life she had also developed a very strong capacity for making the highest pitched scream-bark that anyone has ever heard. We heard it. She was looking for us. We all met in the middle of the park and gave our puppy kisses. Tony was ready to go back to the truck, but not before showing us a good portion of the park by foot. He took us to the rock formations we see a lot of the time in shows like Law & Order, NYPD Blues, and CSI New York. The bridges were gorgeous and I couldn't wait to come back to the park another day with Faith to let her run a bit more, this time with a lot more supervision.

On our first trip to New York City we didn't get to visit all of the places we did the second, third, and forth times. We did however, get to see the Empire State Building, the Statute of Liberty, the largest Post Office, and several studios. We saw David Letterman's studio on Broadway. We saw CNN, ESPN, and some of the shops on Times Square because Tony had some dry cleaning to pick up. He also had a box to deliver, a few errands to run for his wife at a deli he liked better than others, and he always bought his afternoon coffee from the same vendor—had for years. This was New York City. This was what I believed it to be. A maniac driver with a past I'm sure was as scary as I imagined it to be, but with the biggest smile, the best of manners, and the most interesting intimate facts about the city itself. He knew where everything happened, where everyone lived, and what everyone did. I could have driven around with Tony for years.

Two months on the couch

Three months

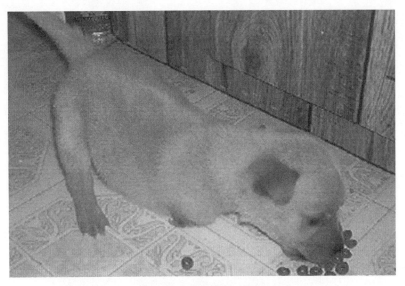

Five weeks old eating

Ten weeks sitting pretty

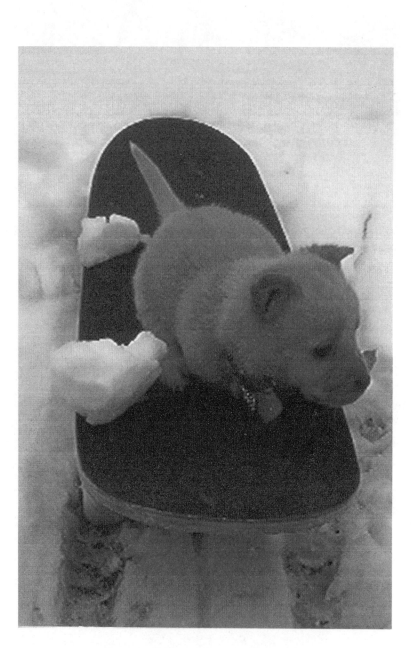

Baby on the board

Caity Baby

Caity with the boys

Faith and Jude

Faith sitting

Internet shot

Kissing

Laura and Faith on the plane

Laura Cakes

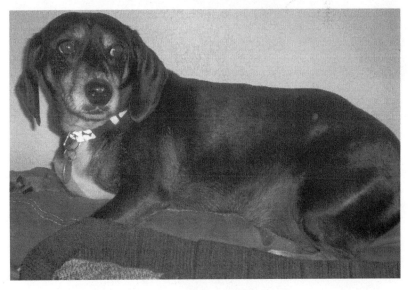

My perfect mutt Matrix

Our Angel

Reuben (92 for Reggie White)

Taking a rest

Walking in the park

# Chapter Eleven

## Maury

I love Maury Povich! The Maury Show is a syndicated talk show that comes on in the mornings and has a certain edge to it. I didn't watch the show that often, but I knew that the man behind the show was brilliant, good looking, fun to be around, and that he loved dogs. His people called us in the winter just after the Ricki Lake Show aired, he wanted Faith on his show too. Everyone wanted Faith. The summer of 2003 she was invited to go to New York City to be on the Today Show for NBC, but the scheduled day for flight ended up being August 14, the day of the biggest blackout in New York City history. We were not allowed to board our plane in Oklahoma City since our final destination was New York City. Other flights had taken off, but we were told no. Perhaps it was because we were traveling with Faith. Too much of the unknown, as it turns out, we have yet to be on the Today Show. However, the day that we arrived in Newark Airport to be taken to our hotel so that we could later be on the Maury Show, we were greeted by a very large, shark-smiling, Italian man, wearing a short-to-the-waist black leather jacket, blunt-toed boots, with a magazine folded in his hand. He was staring straight at us. I leaned over and told Laura that Tony had a hit on us!

What might be of interest to some readers is that on this particular flight a very famous and well known former football player who had played for the New York Giants for years, was on our flight. He and his beautiful wife sat just in front of us in First Class. Over and over again on the flight from Chicago he made the mistake of thinking someone was talking to him when they would ask if they could take a picture. He would turn to them, and before he even saw them, he would be half way through his little speech about how he was not to be disturbed. He was not going to tolerate people coming up to him in flight—he then realized that every time he thought someone was addressing him, they were addressing me. He must have made this mistake four times in the air, and at least six more times in the baggage claim. His wife began laughing at him, and he walked off and left her standing alone in the baggage claim area. I never once declined anyone the opportunity to take a picture of Faith or to get our number so that they could call us later to say hello to the world's most famous dog. I decided not to tell Faith about this man's behavior, I let her go on believing he was great.

This trip Laura and I were accompanied by my younger daughter Caity, who at the time was in love with Orlando Bloom, and thought she saw him every where she looked in the airport. Could that be him? Over there? Tony came up to us, and Caity, who had never met him, recognized him immediately. "Hello Tony!" she said, and he greeted her with the typical nod you see tough guys give to people they know, and I swear—it happened—Tony said "How ya doin'" to Caity. Yes, we were in New York again! Tony's company worked for several studios, and when he saw the ticket for the two-legged dog Faith and her family, he told us he busted up a few guys to get the job, but that he didn't mind, they deserved it. With Tony, we weren't sure if he was telling the truth or joking—we just smiled and laughed, the way Oklahomans do when we don't really know if we should run for the hills or wait it out.

"Have you seen Orlando Bloom?" asked Caity, Tony gave her a one-eyed cocked look and said he would have already run over the kid if he had. Again, we smiled and nodded, just wondering in our hearts if this was part of an act or if this man was the real deal. Tony didn't take us straight to the Skyline Hotel where we were staying, seems he had some business to take care of, so he dropped us off at Times Square for an hour or so, and we didn't care. Up and down the street we walked, freezing our bums off because it was the 10th of February. We managed to buy a hot pretzel, get that afternoon cup of coffee from Tony's favorite vendor before he shooed us off, and then we were off to Quicksilvers, Virgin, MTV, and a few other stores that were just waiting to take our money and see our dog. A man leaving the Virgin Record store on Times Square almost got hit by oncoming traffic as he ran across the street to see Faith. He was about 5'7" and maybe 150 pounds but he jumped straight into the air and on top of the taxi that nearly hit him. He then kicked the windshield of the taxi car, screamed a little something at the driver about watching where he was driving, and gathering himself up, he came across the street with his hands outstretched. "Faith!" he called. He had seen her on something. He recognized her immediately, not that she has much competition in that regard, but it was the first time someone from another area outside our native Oklahoma City had called out her name in public. We were on Times Square in New York City, and here is this man leaping over taxis and dodging death to hug my dog. I was floored when Faith let him pet her. Usually she shies from men, having no defense mechanism. She won't bite, but she won't let men reach out and grab her either. This man did.

Billy Cappoli was his name. He told me so as he shook my hand and I barely got to say hi before being whisked away by the shark-faced man with the leather jacket. Finally, we were at the hotel, about to rest, when all of the sudden an invasion of the British took place. Dozens of them, pouring into the hotel lobby with cameras at the ready, questions flying, ooohs, and ahhhs, fast-talking, Queen's English sort of questions. I managed somewhat, but Laura loved it. Answering each and every one of the visitors who had been told of Faith's arrival. We were suppose to have stayed in the Pennsylvania Hotel, but that hotel was nearly overtaken by the dogs who would be showing off their moxie and good looks the next day for the Westminster Dog Show. These were dozens of furry friend fans who had been told by the Penn that we were staying at the Skyline. The two hotels are literally several miles apart. To think that these people boarded cabs and drove all the way to Hell's Kitchen from the more glamorous area of the city to see Faith was amazing to me. Not to them. They were pleased and thrilled that we allowed pictures, answered questions, and because we weren't bothered with them they offered a great deal of information about a particular film that was about to go into production that two of the mob thought Faith should be a part of. ***Harry Potter and the Goblet of Fire.***

We went on to our room and talked about it. Could it be true? Could one of those people really be from Birds and Animals Inc., the group that provides the training for the animals in the Harry Potter movies? That would be awesome! We decided to relax a bit and see what happened. Tony wasn't picking us up until the morning, so we had plenty of time to rest or go back onto the town to explore the neighborhood. Caity and I were feeling a bit more ambitious than Laura so we took off.

Caity and I strolled down Times Square around 9:00 p.m. and we saw thousands of people who hadn't met Faith in person, or in dog. We must have stopped every five feet to answer the same questions: What happened to her legs? How old is Faith? Does she have any hip problems? What does she do when she needs to go pee? Where are you from? We decided it would be fun to get t-shirts printed up with FAQ printed on the front of the shirt and the answers on the back, but then we'd be spinning around and around and probably getting pretty dizzy by the time we were finished answering everyone's questions. Just as you finish answering one group of people a new group comes up laughing, crying, calling out . . . "Hey, is that the dog on TV?" Well, I'm sure several dogs have been on television, but yes, Faith had been on a few shows by this time, and it was fun to call back "No, that was the other two-legged yellow dog" just to see them laughing and waving back.

One of the things that amazes people about Faith is her smile. She is always laughing or smiling when she sees new people or when we're in the park and she can see a group coming toward her. There's something about her eyebrows, if dogs have eyebrows, that makes her look inquisitive and everyone thinks she's so pretty when she opens up that big mouth of hers and wags her tongue to the side. Because her mother was a Chow, Faith inherited the spotted tongue from her. Her tongue is pink and purple, and everyone notices it. I used to tease younger kids and say that her tongue was moldy. They'd make faces and say "grossssss" and then I'd tell them the truth. Faith's ability to stand up quickly always makes the kids step back and stare, laugh, point, and they call out "Whoa! That's incredible!" which it is. I have to admit, seeing Faith stand up from a completely prone position is quite incredible. She uses her stomach muscles, her leg and thigh muscles, and sometimes, if she is going slowly, she will use her head to sort of pop herself straight up . . . and then she's off!

I won't name names, but when we were in New York City a very famous red-headed actress was going to see the Broadway performance of *The Producers* when she suddenly stopped in her tracks. She saw Faith walking upright, and the tears began to fall. She ran across the traffic to see Faith, and with both hands extended, she wrapped her hands around Faith's face and gave her a big fat kiss on the head. She didn't care about her mascara running, she was just so happy to see Faith. She said her mother had told her that Faith was in town doing a show, but she never thought she would ever see her in person. New York City is just too big she said, but here she was. The media bugs on the sidewalk at the play came by with cameras flashing. I don't think they got a picture of her kissing Faith, but they took several of her standing with Faith. I haven't seen any of the pictures in print, but you never know. I think I asked the actress why she thought Faith was so cool, and her answer was really heart warming. She said that Faith is the one thing in the media that she could think of that wasn't going for money or fame, she just wanted people to realize that everything is possible when you put your heart and mind to it. You don't have to be rich and famous to show off how beautiful you are . . . that's Faith. She doesn't even try hard. Faith just walks around and people are happy. That's the story really, that's the secret if there is one. We give credit to Jesus for all that He did in allowing Faith the courage and strength to pursue what would be normal. If we could all learn to be as strong and have a little faith, we could walk—or believe just as strongly.

The next morning we were picked up by another guy—it wasn't Tony. We ended up riding in a big, black van, and as the guy pulled out into traffic we were nearly side swiped by a taxi that obviously didn't want to slow down to let incoming traffic merge. In New York its nearly impossible to stay in one lane for more than few seconds because the streets are narrow and there are simply too many cars, vans, trucks, and delivery trucks on the streets. Every street is crowded and the endlessness of it makes your head swim if you're not used to it. Here we were, in the van, with the kids and Faith, and a taxi comes from out of no where and just about collides into us. The driver of the taxi honks, gives us a one-fingered salute, and tries to drive off. Our driver, another New York City native, decided to pull out in front of the taxi just enough to make him stop. I'm thinking we're going to be shot, but our driver gets out of his car and bangs both of his hands on the top of the taxi. He speaks Italian to the taxi cab driver and gets back into the van. Not to be outdone, the taxi driver gets out of his car and bends our antenna! I couldn't believe it. Just as the man is about to break the antenna off he looked inside the van to see my shocked face, and a yellow fuzzy dog smiling, wagging her tongue and cocking her head to the side at all the yelling going on outside her door.

The driver of the taxi stopped. The antenna was in his hands. He looked at our driver, and again in Italian he asked if the dog he was driving was Faith. Our driver straightened up a bit, squared his shoulders, shrugged a bit and answered yes, it was Faith, what of it? The taxi driver smiled a tremendously big smile, and apologized three or four times. He smiled, waved at us, sort of fixed the antenna, and got back into his car—allowing us to drive ahead of him. I looked back in the mirror to see the taxi driver pulling out a cell phone, no doubt telling someone who he had just seen on the streets of Hell's Kitchen in New York City!

We got to the Maury Show and our driver didn't waste any time telling the crew what had just happened. It was amazing to see their faces as Faith walked through the studio, around the corners, up the stairs, and onto the stage where Maury Povich spoiled her with kisses and accolades about what a great dog she was. He couldn't believe how happy she was, and he told us off camera that she was much prettier than he thought she had been in the pictures he had seen. He was most impressed with the way she got up from a laying down position and wanted to be sure and get that on film. He did. His show was aired and millions of people were able to see just how wonderful Faith can be with cameras, lights, people, props, stage edges, crowds of people . . . she loves the limelight.

# Chapter Twelve

## On the Streets of New York City

I've told this story before in a book called "With a Little Faith", but it needs to be told again. Faith has such an amazing power that I am not keenly aware of 24/7/365. Sometimes, probably because I live with her, I forget how powerful her message of survival, inspiration and love can be. I think of Faith as my puppy. She's an angel sent from God, and we just love her, spoil her, take her places, and see the faces of everyone when they come in contact with her. However, Faith's story is simply a miracle that unfolds in so many different ways for so many different people. One of those people is a woman that I call Carolyn Gold. Carolyn was a single woman whose children were completely grown. She was, if I remember, about fifty years old and she was restrained to a wheelchair because she had been diagnosed with diabetes a few years back and had recently lost both of her legs to the disease. Because Carolyn was lonely, and now without anyone near her to love her, she had decided that ending her life would be the best decision. She didn't want to be a burden to her family or friends if her condition worsened. She had made the decision a while back, and had even gone so far as to travel by wheelchair down the streets of New York City to a pawnshop where she had purchased a gun. In the state of New York you have to wait a week I think to get the gun after you purchase it. This was the day she was to retrace her steps to the pawn shop and pick up the gun. It was the same day we were on the streets of her city, just shopping and looking for things to take home as souvenirs. Carolyn had watched television that morning and had seen a rerun of the Ricki Lake Show or the Maury Show. I'm not sure which it was. She had called a friend to tell them about Faith perhaps, and was told that Faith was in town. She couldn't believe it. Faith was on the same street that the pawn shop was on. I don't know how long it took Carolyn to find us, probably not too long. In the City people tend to buy from their own neighborhoods, and there are dozens of apartments in the area of Times Square. Against New York City traffic Carolyn Gold wheeled herself to the corner where we were standing. I thought she was going to be hit by cars left and right. A policeman helped get her onto the curb where we were, and I pulled her close to us. She was crying, her face completely wet when she told me her story, and about her decision. She said she was simply not sure she could make it any longer in her condition. Then something happened to Carolyn. She saw Faith. She not only saw Faith, she returned to her own faith.

We were able to put Faith in the lap of this woman, and somehow God told Faith to just lay still, not to move. She sat on Carolyn's lap for several minutes, maybe ten, and Carolyn just cried and loved on her. Because we were causing a bit of a crowd, people with camera phones and tourists with cameras began to gather around us. Pictures were snapped immediately, I think for the first time in her life Carolyn felt like a movie star! She was smiling, laughing, crying, holding onto Faith and just thanking us out loud for being in New York and for raising Faith. I didn't know what to do or what to say. I don't think what we did for Faith was more than what we would have done for any dog or pet that we have ever taken care of. We just did what we thought was right. We let a little dog with bright eyes and an alert face live when maybe she wouldn't have if she had stayed with her mother. Carolyn made another decision that day.

She decided to let the gun stay at the pawn shop. She wasn't going to be using it, and that was the best thing I could have heard on the streets of New York City that day, or probably any other day.

Carolyn is not the only person who has made a decision to keep trying because they have personally met Faith. We were in Grapevine, Texas at an Amerisuites Hotel when we met up with a family that had driven from New Orleans to see Faith. We were doing a show called the Texas Outdoor Expo this past summer. The family found us just before we went out for the second day of the show. We were having breakfast at our hotel when they came in; there were five in the group, all wanting to meet Faith up close and personal. The father was in his fifties. He had his twenty-seven year old son David with him, David's wife Karyn, their child Analynn, and his own wife Cheryl. David had been diagnosed with diabetes just a few months before the show. The disease had been so aggressive that David had already lost his left leg and was having to schedule a trip to Houston to have his right leg removed within the next month and a half. David had decided that he didn't want to live any longer, but his wife Karyn couldn't bear the thought of raising Analynn alone; and she certainly didn't want to be left a widow. She begged David to drive to Dallas/Grapevine to meet Faith. She said if he didn't change his mind about living she would understand, but she really wanted him to meet the dog that walked upright and made such a difference in so many people's lives. Karyn had purchased my book and had read Carolyn Gold's story. It reminded her of David's decision, and she was able to talk him into meeting Faith. Interestingly, or perhaps it was fate, we were scheduled to be in Grapevine the week before he was to show up for his surgeon's interview.

We were in the hotel dining room when they came in. At first they stopped by the front desk to ask if we were still in the hotel. They must have timed it just right, we were eating breakfast and would be leaving for the show within thirty minutes. When David saw us he immediately hung his head. He began to shake a little and I noticed that he reached up for Karyn's hand. She knelt beside him and in silence we all just sort of stared at each other. Analynn, being two, screamed out "Dog!" as loud as she could, and came giggling and running up to the yellow mutt she found so pretty. Faith, for her part, popped up on queue, ran around the dining room to get away from the charging little girl, but in the end, she was caught. We held her close, and helped Analynn with her petting skills. Faith is after all a dog, and we didn't want there to be any accidents. Faith allowed Analynn to pet and hug her a bit before walking over to David, who was reaching out his hand to be sniffed.

It has always been OK for men to cry, and therefore, when David began crying I couldn't stop myself from letting tears fall. Karyn hugged me before she had even introduced herself, and no introduction was needed, I knew from the wheelchair, the tears, the family holding onto each other, and the way the silence rang heavy in the room that this was one of those miracle moments that only God can coordinate. His timing is simply amazing to me. How a little yellow dog, popping up and running around a room trying her best to get away from a toddler can do so much for everyone is just mind blowing. David and Karyn, mom, dad, my girls, and I just sat at the tables watching Analynn with her new friend. Karyn explained the story to me as I nodded quietly. I couldn't actually relate personally, but having been with Carolyn at the moment she saw Faith, I understood what it was that David was feeling. He didn't feel that he was able to go on, and he wanted it all to end. Facing a difficulty like his is devastating. I don't know what I would do if I were in his place, but for grace we are all in his place at one time or another. If having a little dog to share with someone is all I am asked to do, I will do it all day long as long as I can.

# Chapter Thirteen

## Montel Williams

Montel Williams in my opinion, is the best looking man in New York City! Not only was he a gracious host, his staff proved to be the best in the business, treating us with the greatest of love and respect. Our time with Montel and his staff was truly a highlight of our many trips to our favorite home away from home. I often tell my children and friends that if I could I would have an apartment in New York City just above one of the over 100 Starbucks in Manhattan alone. So far my favorite building is 45 Wall Street, which of course, has a Starbucks on the ground floor. Montel's studio is located at 433 W. 53$^{rd}$ in the City, and is easily accessed from Time Square, Rockefeller Center, Central Park, and just a brisk walk away from the Empire State Building.

On this trip to the City I took my son Reuben. It was Reuben's first time to the Big Apple, as the city is called, and he was absolutely flattened by the sites. One of the first things to happen to us when we arrived was hilarious, and again, if it hadn't been for Faith, things could have gotten ugly. Because Reuben is such a normal kid, at the time I think he was nineteen, just out of high school, getting ready for college and being an average guy on the streets—a tourist. Reuben and I were walking up and down the streets and avenues when Reu spotted a giant statue in the shape of a sphere, the world I think. In an instant my son was jumping up on the platform of the statue and asking me to take his picture. Immediately five of New York City's Finest were blowing whistles and running toward my son. Seems you can't jump on the platforms of statues in this particular city. It makes sense. You have a city of more than ten million people it stands to reason that public property should be respected a bit more than what my son was showing. Within seconds the cops stopped—started calling out, laughing, and saying "Hey, it's Faith!" They had recognized her from one of the many times we were on television or perhaps walking their beat. We try to stop and say hi to every single fire fighter and cop we can in every city we visit. Reu was scolded, but allowed to live another day, and we talked a while with the guys, took some pictures, and told a few good stories. We even got an escort from two of them who wanted us to walk up "their" street to meet up with a few more buddies who hadn't seen Faith in a while. Coffee is always free in cases like this, and in Manhattan there's a store on every corner with a big green circle hosting a swimming mermaid. I love Starbucks.

On the Montel Show Faith was one of several animals that were being featured for their amazing feats in life. There was Zeke, a beautiful collie in Texas that saved his owner's life when her breathing monitor went out. We shared the stage with Titan, a giant chocolate Labrador that literally pulled his mommy from a pool when she hit her head on the concrete. We were privileged to be with a little white poodle dog that brought his owner, a little boy, a kiss of life when he was about to die. The little dog kept barking and licking his owner until he regained consciousness, and we were also in the presence of a woman whose elder cat smelled smoke and alerted the family to sure danger. These were amazing animals; and we even met a parrot that had over 500 words in her vocabulary. So, you might ask why was Faith on the show? Well, turns out she was nominated by a viewer because she was an incredible pet simply because she had learned to overcome overwhelming obstacles. Faith hasn't saved us from a burning house, or pulled anyone from a pool, but she has overcome so much in her life that people see her as an inspiration because of her tenacity, hard work, and faith in herself. I'm not sure if dogs or cats can have faith in God, or if they pray, but I'm sure that God has a plan for animals. They bring such love and happiness into our lives when we need it, love so unconditional, so unattached or without strings, that we humans could truly learn from their ability to just open up their hearts and accept us for who we are. I often tell people that I want to be the person that my dog Matrix thinks that I am. I would be the best person in the entire world if that would happen. We have to remember that dogs (and probably some cats) love humans because we care for them, we love them; even people who don't love people will love animals—usually.

Montel was taken back by the way Faith walked on his stage. He smiled and held back a laugh when he saw her wagging that tongue. She obliged him by standing up from a laying position, and then she walked around his stage checking out the decorations he had behind the chairs we sat in for the interview. No doubt she was probably looking for a piece of bacon or cheese. She could smell it from one of the green rooms where we were waiting before the show. Because shows like the Montel Williams Show are taped and then edited, Faith was allowed to burp on stage and have it dubbed out. I saw Montel's face when she burped. His eyebrows raised and he laughed. I am sure several people sitting in the audience could hear it too. I don't know if the boom microphones were still on, but it was actually dubbed out of the show when it aired in February 2006. A dog's gotta do what a dog's gotta do. I try telling people that Faith is like any other dog, the only difference is, she has learned to walk upright, loves cameras and bright lights, and from time to time she will steal food from the hands of anyone not really paying attention. She is a dog. A fantastic, wonderful, miracle, and amazing dog, but she is a dog. She reminds us of this fact nearly every day, and we love her for it.

# Chapter Fourteen

## Chicago Take One

Coming home from the Montel Williams Show was no where near as easy as arriving. Weather had hampered our departure, and we were unable to take off when we landed in Chicago for a connecting flight. We were asked to stay overnight, and American Airlines found us a hotel to stay in. Getting to the terminal exits was a task in an of itself, limited electricity in the airport made it virtually impossible to open doors that normally opened automatically, and we couldn't take elevators or escalators to the floors or areas we needed to get to. In fact, finding a shuttle from our terminal to the hotel meant that we had to physically walk about two blocks in the airport and another two blocks outside to find the shuttle that eventually took us to the hotel. The driver of the shuttle tried to warn us that the Holiday Inn near Chicago's O'Hare Airport did not take dogs. We believed (wrongfully) that because American Airlines had booked our reservation, that the agent at the gate clearly knew we were traveling with a dog, was better informed. She was not. We arrived at the hotel about twenty minutes after departing the airport. We were greeted at the door by strong winds and freezing temperatures, not to mention the snow that was falling and the ice that paved the entrance to the hotel itself.

The manager of the hotel met us from behind the counter with a shaking of his head. He was not going to allow us to stay in his hotel with Faith. We argued of course, stating that American had made the reservations, but he was not going to budge in his decision. Almost immediately following the discussion as to whether or not we were going to be able to stay, a nice couple came out of the bar just to the side of the lobby. "Is this Faith" they wanted to know. Finally, I thought, the manager will see that Faith is not an ordinary dog, and he will allow the stay. That didn't happen. As the couple found themselves laying on the floor to take pictures so Faith didn't have to stand, another man came out of the hallway with his luggage and wanted to know if Faith was indeed the same Faith that he had seen on several shows. She was we assured him. He was pleased to be able to have met Faith—he was traveling from California, but was an English gentlemen on business. He stayed many times at this particular Holiday Inn, and had a long standing reservation with them whenever he pleased. He was upset that the hotel would not honor the airlines decision, and questioned the manager as to why he had not confirmed with the airlines that a dog was indeed coming to the hotel that evening. There must have been a mention of it since the agent was the one that booked the reservation while we were standing in front of her gate.

Nevertheless, the manager of the hotel absolutely refused to allow us to stay, and there was not a thing we could do. I didn't have any cash on me, it was in my bag which was probably in the belly of some plane going to Oklahoma City without me. I had a bank card, but this particular hotel didn't take debit cards, and without a very sizable deposit we were without hope. I asked the manager is he actually intended to put us out on the streets with the temperature hovering in single digits. His answer was yes, he was. Amazing! The thought of a hotel manager even thinking of placing a family and an animal for that matter out in such conditions flabbergasted me. It must have made an impression on my new English friend Lyndon Smith as well. He pulled out his credit card, a platinum card, and he paid for my deposit, Faith's deposit, as I assume the extra money was not necessary for human customers. We thanked him, and promised to pay him back, but I lost his address and was unable to do so. I asked American Airlines to reimburse him, or to send him frequent flyer miles, but to this day I don't know that they have. I hope so, he was an angel. People never cease to amaze and astound me with the way they respond to Faith's needs. Faith had no idea that she was causing such a problem by being a dog, but it was because she was a dog that Mr. Smith was deeply moved to help us. She was a miracle dog he had seen on television and had been touched by her strength and courage.

Since the event at the Holiday Inn near Chicago I have stayed at several other Holiday Inns and Holiday Inn Express hotels that do accept dogs without question. I do hope that every Holiday Inn will take a lesson from the story and be a bit more kind to guests who have no control over weather conditions, and are at the mercy of the gate agents booking their reservations. Still I am reminded that the shuttle driver knew the policies of his hotel. He tried to warn us. I suppose we could have stayed overnight in the dark, cold, scary, airport with limited electricity, but as it worked out—I am glad we were in soft comfortable beds with a complimentary pizza for dinner. Our next trip to Chicago, or rather Faith's next trip to Chicago, would prove to be so much nicer.

# Chapter Fifteen

## Inside Edition, PBS and Oprah!

In the spring of 2006, Faith had been asked to be televised by several shows including Inside Edition, ET, and the Oprah Show. We were unable to do anything with Entertainment Tonight, but look forward to doing something in the future should they call. Inside Edition however, was another story. They came to my city so that they could shoot an interview, and film what is called "B-Roll" footage of Faith running around outside, playing in a park, just sitting around, and being a natural dog. The person interviewing me sat opposite of me off camera, and she asked me several questions that many of the viewers of the show have written in to ask, or what we would call frequently asked questions. She went a bit further, and asked a few questions that most people want to know but maybe have a reservation about asking. I am always happy to answer questions regarding Faith because people are genuinely curious, and they simply want to know the answers without it being a big deal. I appreciated the candidness of the interviewer, and tried my hardest to answer as best I could. The only thing that upset me was that they interviewed both Caity and Reuben and then didn't put them on air, which was sad because Laura and I seem to get all of the attention.

Faith is actually Laura's dog. Matrix is my dog. He's perfect in every way. I tell him this over and over, and I think it's beginning to sink in. Laura became Faith's rightful owner after Reuben moved out of our house after saving her from her own mother. Reuben couldn't take Faith with him, and he would not have been effective in raising her alone, therefore he gave her to Laura to keep. Caity had Ean, the Corgi that bit Faith and taught her how to run. We each had our own dogs to love and care for. We didn't know at that time that owning Faith would demand a life change for all of us, but it happened, and we're OK with it. Being Faith's people is fine with us. We're up to the challenge.

When the Inside Edition coverage ran we began getting phone calls from other countries to do shows and interviews as well. Seems Inside Edition is worldwide, and people on four continents called us within weeks of the release of the footage. We did telephone and internet interviews with people in Australia, Europe, North America and South America. I'm still waiting for people in Africa to call and say that they have seen us on Inside Edition as well. Perhaps that will happen someday. Because we used my friend Trudy's house to showcase our interview, I felt it was only best to borrow it again when the crew came by to film the B-roll for Oprah.

Oprah's people called us when we were filming Animal Attractions for a PBS-TV station called Pine Ridge out of Jacksonville, Florida. I can't tell you how excited we were to do this show. Animal Attractions was one of the best pieces ever filmed about Faith because it went into more detail about what she means to us now, and what we were like before we had the opportunity to raise her. Before Faith came into our lives we were getting over the troubles and complications that come from a nasty divorce. Americans are quite used to hearing about divorces, and the trials, court house appearances, and the trouble that one or the other spouse can cause the other during these types of proceedings. We were no different, but it was worse in our case, in that my kids were taken from me by an error of the court, and it took a great deal of time to reverse the decision of the court in order to bring them back to me. It was nearly five years from the time we filed for divorce to when I was given full and complete custody of the girls. This was the situation we were in when Reuben found Faith. It was a situation of trying to make the bad feelings go away, trying to rebuild our family through love and prayer. Pine Ridge, or Animal Attractions (Episode 102) made it possible for us to tell that side of the story to the viewers. It also allowed me to talk a little about the book I wrote that showcases the lives we lived before and after we were given Faith. After reading the book, hundreds of people have e-mailed me to say that Faith is not only a miracle worker for them, but that she started her miracle-career at home with us. They couldn't be more correct. We thank God for her so often.

We were wrapping up the filming for Animal Attractions in Florida when the call came from the producer of the Oprah Show saying that they wanted to meet with me at my house, which of course meant borrowing Trudy's house. We met about a week later, and filmed the B-roll interview showing Faith outside with Caity and Laura in several public places. We shot at the pet store, we went to a Starbucks, and even to a local library where we were able to sit in an oversized chair in the children's section and read a few books to some patrons who just happened to be in the library at that time. They were beautiful. Three siblings sitting around the chair, talking, giggling, reading, and petting Faith. She kicked back and enjoyed herself while the kids read to her, something we are pleased to be able to do when we can. Faith is not a R.E.A.D. dog, R.E.A.D. stands for Reading Education Assistance Dog. We are not affiliated with this organization, but we do about the same thing that they do. We allow Faith to be read to by students, or just people, who would otherwise feel embarrassed to read out loud. I am a teacher, and some of my students asked to read to Faith rather than to me, because I must have had a judgmental face when they missed a word, or perhaps mispronounced a word. Faith doesn't judge anyone. She has no reason to tell someone that they have misquoted, mispronounced, or even that they may have skipped a line or two in their reading. She just sits back, listens, and occasionally sighs when they are reading to her. From time to time she will roll over and demand that the reader pet her belly at the same time he or she is reading, this I am sure she does to see if they can concentrate on two separate issues. She's smart like that.

So, here we were filming the B-roll for the Oprah Show and I remember telling Laura not to worry about saying anything to Oprah personally because the producers had asked me to be on stage rather than Laura. I always try my best to get Laura on stage or in front of the cameras because Faith is actually her dog, but believe it or not, people say they prefer adults telling stories—I find that odd, but it is true. On the very day I was to fly with the girls and Faith to Chicago to be on the Oprah Show, I became too ill to fly. I didn't have a chance in Heaven of making it on board that plane, and we had to reschedule the flight for a later time in the day in hopes that my migraine headache would go away. It never went away. Later in the afternoon however, I found myself driving ever so slowly to the airport with the girls and Faith, spewing out instructions to Laura who was now going to be face to face with the greatest television hostess in the world within a few hours. Laura wasn't nervous at first. As time began to run out and Laura realized that I really wasn't going to be getting on the plane with her, she admitted that she may have to instruct Caity on how to speak to the greatest television hostess in the world in just a few hours. Caity was about to explain to Faith how to conduct an interview alone, when Laura pulled herself up by her own bootstraps and began practicing on the airplane what she would actually say to Oprah.

Arriving very late the night before the show, Laura, Caity and Faith were whisked away to the Omni Hotel, which was by far the grandest hotel any of them had stayed in. They were picked up by limousine, fed well, and told to be perky and on the move by about 6:45 the next morning, or actually in about four and a half hours. They were ready. Green tea energy drinks in hand, fruit and bran cakes crammed down them, both girls and the dog were being taken to the stage, dressed, attended to, and finally instructed on what they were to say to Oprah when she asked them questions. Oprah was taken by utter surprise when she first saw Faith, and the moment Faith walked onto her stage, the greatest hostess of television—cried. She held her hand over her mouth for a second, and then over her heart. She repeated the words "I've never, I've never, I've never" several times, as Faith strutted her stuff across the stage and made her way with Laura to the two chairs positioned in the center of the stage. To Oprah's surprise again, Faith stood up and tried to leave the stage when she recognized Caity sitting directly in front of her.

Not all of the questions that were to be discussed had been made clear to Laura, and one question that Laura truly expected to be asked never was. Laura handled herself very well on stage, answering why Faith's tongue was spotted, telling Oprah about Faith being a R.E.A.D. dog, which we know she isn't. Laura was a bit nervous, and she explained to Oprah the way students from another country, in this case Mexico, learn to read to Faith when they would be otherwise embarrassed to read out loud to a teacher. The audience was completely taken not only by the B-roll footage that showed the various stages of Faith's life in chronological order, but also with the way she behaved herself with cameras and lights, booms, and people all around her. She's at home on a stage. We often joke about putting fake cameras and lights in our house just to make Faith feel good when she comes in from a trip around the neighborhood.

The show we were chosen to be on with Oprah was filmed May 18, 2006, and shown the very next day. It was a show of incredible odds, and this time everyone else on the show was a human. A little 8-year old boy had been nearly killed by his father. His mother had been murdered in front of his own eyes, and the little boy was so brave and so strong at his young age, he managed to call 9-1-1 on his own and have the police come to his rescue. A teacher with Tourette syndrome had managed to not only teach his class year after year, he became Teacher of the Year! There was also a man who had been climbing a mountain and had a huge boulder fall on his legs. They were crushed, and eventually, after a miraculous life saving adventure, his legs were removed. That did not stop him from continuing his life in an ordinary, or extraordinary manner. He continues to climb today. I'm always taken by the fact that people equate what Faith has done with these types of achievements. She is a miracle, no doubt, but it is a bit humbling when I realize she's just the little yellow dog that lies under my bed every day and begs me for my dinner each night. Somehow, I know she's more than just a little yellow dog, but she's so close to me all of the time that it's hard to see the trees for the forest at times.

When the Oprah show aired and re-aired in re-runs people came up to us in hotels, restaurants, on the street, in the airports, everywhere and asked if Faith was the same dog they had just seen on the Oprah Show. We affirm that she is, but sometimes just for fun we say "No, that was her twin, this is Hope", they never believe us. Which is a good thing. We shouldn't tease Faith like that, if she only knew. Oprah has posted Faith's appearance on her website, and has listed my book "With a Little Faith" on her books seen in the month of May 2006 on the internet. If you ever get a chance to meet Oprah in person, or to go see her show, you should do so. She is one of the most gracious, and inspirational women I have ever been associated with. I only wish I wasn't ill the day I was to fly to Chicago. Perhaps another day we will meet up and laugh about it. I know Faith liked her, and she proudly wears the bumblebee collar gifted to her by Oprah and her staff.

# Chapter Sixteen

## Traveling with the World Famous Dog Faith

You get the phone call or the e-mail asking you to show up at a certain time to do an interview, or to be televised, but there are so many things that must take place first. Faith is probably not the only dog in the world that has ridden up in the front of the cabin of the plane with her owners. I'm sure there are many, in fact we know one—Tyson the Skateboarding Bulldog rides up in the cabin with his mom and dad. Getting a dog inside the plane takes some doing. First, because Faith has celebrity status she must be booked with her celebrity status by the travel agent or else she will be booked as an ordinary pet. Ordinary pets don't have their own seats. If they stay in the crates they may be allowed to sit on the floor of the plane in front of their owners, but they are not allowed to be free or capable of roaming, as Faith often does when we are on extended flights.

Flying with Faith can be fun, but it can be difficult if the booking is incorrect and I have to stand in line a good deal longer allowing for phone calls to be made, arrangements, and so forth. I used to make the arrangements myself, but after the booking agent at the airlines made mistakes I didn't want to be held responsible for not showing up on time—I now let the host of whoever is bringing us out make all of the reservations. I am always available for suggestions.

The first thing I say is to call American Airlines because Faith has flown so often with them that they all but recognize her name, and she is usually booked without any problems as a celebrity, and not a pet. In order for a pet to be given celebrity status on American Airlines they must meet criteria that is written out in the American Airlines manual. We had one problem, one time, while on flight with the criteria. Can you guess the flight? That's right, the same flight that booked us inappropriately in Chicago at the Holiday Inn near airport, was the only flight that questioned Faith's celebrity status and threatened to have us taken off the airplane. Since that time Faith has flown more than a dozen times with American and I have a hard copy written form from one of the Captains stating that he doesn't want to hear of any problems with the crew at any junction. It states that Faith flies "all of the time" and that she is to be treated as "the celebrity that she is". This makes me feel really good, and I have to admit, a little special, when we are boarded first, or through doors usually reserved for movie stars, or public figures such as politicians and heads of state.

On one flight out of Dallas (I would be hard pressed to remember where we were going, we go through Dallas so often), Faith sat down in her chair, 7D of the Super 80 plane we were booked on, and she began sniffing people as they passed by her. We are often boarded early to have time to get her seated, strapped in, and have our carry on luggage stowed before the other passengers pass. She began sniffing one man in particular and she sort of barked when he stood beside her. Her nose pressed hard against the side of his pant leg. I must admit, I was a bit embarrassed. I pulled her back, gave him a slight smile, and tried to divert her attention. She would not be detoured however. She persisted in sniffing him, barking a little louder, and finally he pushed her away himself. When he did she somewhat nipped at him. It made me wonder. The man ended up sitting a row or two behind us, and I wrote a little note to the flight attendant because Faith had never been that interested in a passenger's pant before. When the flight attendant returned to me a few minutes later she whispered in my ear that the man had been carrying a joint in his lower leg pocket. It wasn't much, but enough for Faith to notice and she asked him to flush the joint before he left the plane. I wondered if she told him she would have him pass by Faith again just to be sure. I did notice that he had gotten out of his seat during the flight, and he was shaking his head smiling. Who knew? Faith could actually have an entirely different career if she needed to. As a teacher we have drug dogs coming into our schools and classrooms. It dawned on me that most of them were Labradors too. Faith's father may very well be part Lab because not only is she a natural drug dog, she chases geese all the way into the water before realizing that she doesn't swim well enough to get out on her own. We always say her father is a handsome, yellow fence-jumper.

When she is flying on the plane, or actually riding in the plane when it is flying through the air, Faith is very quiet. Even when the engines groan, and the air is bumpy, she just lies there and sighs. Sometimes she will try to sleep and other times she likes to listen to the kids on the plane as they giggle and make noise closer to the back. Every once in a while, if the flight attendants don't mind, she will get up and walk around the front half of the plane and accept peanuts or treats from people curious enough to crane their necks forward (or backward from First Class) to see her. When we fly on CRJ70 jets we are in the first row, there is no First Class, and Faith is able to stay up front with the flight attendants a little more often.

One such trip, recently taken from Cleveland to Dallas was one of the best trips ever. Tito and Shane were our flight attendants, both very handsome young men, one taller than the other, perfectly balanced in humor, and very neat, pristine, and quite the comedians on board. While searching for a magazine to read on board Tito found a Modern Bride and made a few off-the-cuff jokes about being one, and then decided he would forever give up the magazine to a blushing beauty on board who thought she would make a better Modern Bride. Everyone on the plane was laughing, and Faith was no exception. When she sees people laughing it perks her ears a bit, and she opens that mouth and begins to smile. Shane noticed how big her mouth was and made a comment, to which Tito, without missing a beat, came back with a comment I don't remember, but it set off the plane once more in laughter. These two could certainly take their show on the road, but they do such a great job in the air!

Again in Dallas, everything happens in Dallas, we were scheduled to fly home to Oklahoma City when the doors to the boarding hall of the gate opened and out came a female flight attendant named Lynn. She was pretty, about forty, small in stature and dressed impressively in her blue dress, hose and heels. Instantly she began looking around the gate area, she had been told that Faith the Two-Legged Dog was outside the gate waiting to board her plane once it landed. I'm not sure flight attendants are suppose to exit the craft before the customers do, but Lynn flew off the plane and into the gate area where we were. She went to her knees immediately, asked if she could hug Faith, which was something she was already in the process of doing, and she began to cry. It was her birthday—she had been in Chicago, and had been told that Faith was coming from another city to Dallas to fly home, and rather than taking a paid flight to work a leg through Chicago to Newark. Lynn flew in uniform as a regular passenger to Dallas to see Faith for what amounted to about seven minutes. She was so happy. We took pictures, and we sent them to her. She and her husband took a trip to Italy to see his parents soon after she met with us, and she told everyone about Faith and about all the fun things she has seen Faith do on television. To her surprise, she e-mailed me later, they had seen Faith on many shows that are syndicated and televised in their country. They were jealous she told me, that she was able to see Faith in person . . . or in dog.

Faith usually remains very quiet when she is in the plane and we are flying. She doesn't make a sound, not a word from her, not a noise. It's actually quite easy to forget you are even traveling with her until someone wakes you and asks to take a picture. Sure we say, we never stop people from taking her picture. If that makes them happy, we let them snap a few pictures. There was one time that a picture I gave to someone ended up on a bunch of T-shirts for sale, and that was a problem, but we settled it quickly and because Faith is a trade mark, most people don't try and take advantage of her image. Faith's behavior changes somewhat—well, a great deal—when we land and she can smell her boy Reuben, Caity, Laura, Pop, Grandma, or someone who did not take that particular trip with us. The usually docile, sweet, quiet, little dog becomes loud, barking with a shrill cry and she doesn't stop even when she is in the arms of the person she was barking for. Talk about disruption! SCREEAMMINGGGG couldn't be louder . . . . people stop, stare, point, laugh, get out of her way . . . the dog is on a mission at this point. But in the air . . . peace.

# Chapter Seventeen

## Military Bases—Hospitals—Shows

We began taking Faith to stages early in her life through demonstrating her power to heal emotionally. We were invited to local churches at first, and to counselor's meetings, church-oriented meetings with youth groups, or individual counseling sessions where kids had opened up to their counselors that they felt depressed and unable to make it in life. Faith would show up unexpectedly and give the person a reason to hope, showing them that she was wearing the biggest smile even if she didn't have arms to reach out and hold them with. She couldn't "shake" their hand, but she could certainly shake up their hearts and show them that no one can take that joy away from you if you don't let them have it. Angel Tree is an organization in Bethany, Oklahoma put on by the Bethany First Nazarene Church each year. It is a benefit, non-profit organizations that gives out presents at Christmas time to kids whose parents are in prison for whatever reason and they may not be able to receive the love and care they would receive if their parents were home to hold them during the Christmas season. Faith was invited to perform at one of these events, and she was received so well that they invited her back again and again. Faith and I truly love going to see children in need, because it is what I believe she was created for. She may not be bigger than their problems, but she can help them feel that they can overcome most of the bad, and let God have the control of their lives long enough to become stronger and to be able to face obstacles that would ordinarily be unbearable. If a little dog can do it, if God would do this for a little dog—He can do it for a kid.

We have traveled with Faith to so many shows and as mentioned the Angel Tree was one of her first. On the day of the first show she ever did, we were asked to do a little speaking bit about how we got Faith. I was suppose to say what makes her special, and tell how she is going to be used to make people feel better. I talked a bit about how life is hard and how God uses people and sometimes an animal to make it easier to understand what you are going through. I was planning my speech, setting up the outline in fact, when a little boy came up to me and asked me what my dog's name was. I told him her name was Faith. He told me that his mommy's name was Faith too. His mommy had been put in jail, but he told me that she loved him anyway. I knew she must love her baby, and I told him that I thought so. He asked if Faith had a mommy and I told her that no, she didn't have a mommy anymore, Laura was her human mommy and that I was sort of like a grandma to her. He smiled and then he pet Faith on the head, he whispered in her ear that he would ask Santa to bring Faith a new mommy to love her, a dog mommy. This was so sweet, and it reminded me of the way kids think—not the way adults deal, but the way kids deal with loss. Here his mother was locked away, but he loved her, and he knew she loved him. This little boy thought more of Faith than he did himself that Christmas, wanting to ask Santa for a gift for her; there is just something unselfish about little kids and Faith brings that out in many of them.

An eleven-year old girl at Ft. Lewis, Washington wanted to know if she should go to college and find a cure for Faith. I told her that she was really sweet to think this, but that there wasn't a cure for losing your front legs at birth. Faith wouldn't walk with medal legs, or use a cart. She prefers to walk upright. I told her that when the time comes for Faith to learn to use a cart one would be provided for her. The little girl was sure-faced and she told me that she was going to go to college and build Faith the best cart in the world. I accepted that offer.

We go to military bases like Ft. Lewis, an Army base near Seattle, in order to show the military families how Faith walks by any means possible. Most of the time we are invited to the bases at the time that the men and women of the base are being deployed to go overseas. We have been to Ft. Lewis, Ft. McChord, Tinker Air Force Base, and Carswell in Ft. Worth, Texas so far. We are scheduled to appear at more than six bases this year alone and will continue to meet with Patrick McGhee at the PX in Ft. Lewis to receive our "orders" to appear at other places. Sadly, we were unable to do a show in San Antonio this past summer due to scheduling problems, but we will, and we hope to make it to Walter Reed soon as well. When we go to these places we usually pass out flyers about my book *With a Little Faith Second Edition.* Sometimes the store has ordered several hundred copies and I sit at a little desk signing books while the girls and Reuben field questions all day about Faith, how she walks, her hips, her age, how we got her, and what type of dog she is. Something else that happened at Ft. Lewis that is simply out of this world happened too: Faith was commissioned a Sergeant in the United States Army! She was celebrated, and given her full commission in front of hundreds of spectators at the Madigan Army Medical Center. She has stripes and everything! I know that Privates in the Army don't really have to salute Sergeants, but I do ask Reuben to salute Faith from time to time. She likes it.

Most recently, on a trip to Cleveland to meet with the Greyhound Adoption of Ohio at a really exciting event called the Canine Fun Days, Faith and Laura became overwhelmed when hundreds of people approached them all at once. Laura was literally taken back by the crowd, physically cornering she and Faith. Laura began to field questions and I noticed her big brown eyes widening and actually glazing over at times—she was scared. We decided to back off a bit from the all-access approach and put Laura and Faith behind a little fence where Laura could be a little more assured that she would not be harmed, or that Faith would not be mulled by the crowd. The next day I designed a FAQ fact sheet of frequently asked questions to pass out to the approaching crowds to begin reading while a few people were being spoken to and some of the same questions were answered one on one. Patti and Ron Hetzel, a couple from a nearby town, were there to help us too. Patti and Ron own a gorgeous golden Lab/Retriever mix named Goldie, and they sat with us under the tent for literally two full work days, not being paid, just answering questions and asking a few of their own. I have to tease Ron a bit because I was wearing a light blue T-shirt the first day with a big insignia of Oklahoma University (OU) right in the middle of the shirt when he asked me where I was from. "Oklahoma" I answered, and pulled the shirt up a bit for him to see. He smiled politely, hugged Patti and stated that he doesn't look at women's chests very often, so he wasn't to be blamed for not knowing. Good save Ron!

At the Fun Days we encountered a few odd ball spectators, but for the most part we met thousands of people who loved their dogs with all of their hearts. The Greyhound Reunion was going on too, and most of the proceeds of the Fun Days was actually being donated to the Greyhound Adoption of Ohio. There were t-shirts, cups, novelties, and scarves to buy of course, funnel cakes, cookies, cakes, ice-cream, burgers, fries, and cokes, there were tents lined up on both sides of the main street, and loud rock n' roll music blaring right outside our front tent. We loved every minute of it. As I mentioned earlier in the book, Tyson the Skateboarding Bulldog rides up front in the plane's cabin like Faith, and we found this out because Tyson was one of the main attractions of the Canine Fun Days! He was absolutely gorgeous, bigger than imagined, he was taller, stout, full of life, and believe it or not he has the best looking bum I've seen on a dog. Yes, the boy has cowlick swirls on either side of his butt-cheeks, and they stand out so well with the color of his fur. He can be looked up on the internet, and Faith felt so honored to have met his acquaintance. They hit it off immediately, nosing each other, walking around together, talking in dog language: Tyson snorts, Faith pants a little, and they found each other to be quite interesting. Tyson liked his skateboard, let me tell you. We were given a free demonstration at the WEWS Channel 5 News Station on August 18, 2006 with anchors Alicia Booth, Jack Marschall, and Account Executive Greg Miller. Tyson's dad Jim set Tyson's favorite skateboard down in the studio, and wham! Tyson jumped on it, rolled it out of the area, retrieved it, brought it back in his mouth, grunting and snorting the entire time. He danced around that board, wanting to ride it, but there wasn't enough room in the studio. We had to go out on the front sidewalk, but when we did, boy or boy, Tyson is one good skater! He puts Tony Hawk to shame, I'm sorry, Tony, you're good, but the dog steals the show! Tyson was hot! Everyone wanted to be there, and they came out of the station in droves with cameras and even a remote camera to take footage of this great entertainer. If Faith had things her way, she and Tyson would be best friends forever. Alas, he lives on the West Coast and she in the Southwest . . . love remains in their hearts I'm sure.

The Canine Fun Days was an excellent way for people to meet Faith up close and personal as we tried to be as accessible as possible without freaking the dog out too badly. She was rewarded for her efforts by any and everyone who brought food to the tent. We won't tell her vet about all the burgers, fries, ice cream, and peanut butter cups she was given, what he doesn't know won't hurt him, and from what I saw on the grass the next day, it didn't hurt Faith either. Everything passed just fine. I think she ate a few bites of the Pedigree dog food that the organization brought her, she was full of hamburgers and cheese mostly. I understand completely why Faith is up and ready to attend as many of these events as she can possibly stand to go to in a week.

Whenever we attend events out of state and away from home, Matrix is the first to suffer. He is usually aware of our departure when he spies us getting our bags ready. He has yet to be invited to our gigs, but there is a reason for it. We leave Matrix at home to guard the Chihuahuas and the cat, who I am sure would tear the place up if they were left unattended. Also, who would watch Reuben in case of a thunderstorm, or worse, should a party suddenly break out in my house while we are gone? Yes, Matrix has a very responsible position, he understands his lot in life, and he accepts his mission with pride and complete resign. When we return we are always greeted at the door with love, hugs, and wiggling bodies as the dogs and cat find their way between our feet and under our suitcases vying for positions in which they will establish themselves to be loved as soon as possible. I often wonder what poor Matrix would do if he were asked to attend one of these events. Not being properly trained to fly he would be asked to stay in the cargo area or in a crate, however, because he is perfectly overweight by a few pounds, he would not be allowed in the cabin. His would be a very different experience, and because of that we are happy to allow him to guard the Chihuahuas and the cat as well as my house and son. He is after all, perfectly suited for this task, he is half Dachshund and half Beagle—therefore, Matrix is perfect.

Some of the greatest thrills we receive with Faith come from our visits to the hospitals where we see patients that are about to go through chemotherapy. We are asked to wait until the patient is ready and prepared to go into the room where they will receive their treatment, and sometimes they ask us to wait until after it is administered so that the patient can return and touch Faith again before returning to their room. They rarely speak to us after their treatments, they're either too weak, or sometimes completely out—but they know she is there, and they reach out to her and quietly pet her. She has never been afraid of anyone that is having a treatment. Where sometimes Faith can be shy of men, somehow she has never been shy around a cancer patient, even the men. This has to be Jesus, because in any healthy situation she often hides from men or just walks away from them.

Hospitals can be scary places for some people, and I imagine they can be scary places to dogs since dogs can sense smells, emotions, fear, and anger on people. Dogs are incredibly good at detecting smells of apprehension, confusion, frustration, and fear; so being at a hospital could be a scary place for a dog that wasn't prepared to give love and respect to the patient that is going in for some sort of treatment. An E.R. wouldn't be the best place to find a therapy dog because often times the E.R. is a place of immediate need or even panic. There are areas in a hospital where life can be pretty mundane for patients who are there for longer periods of time while they are trying to recuperate from disease or recover from an accident. Faith doesn't go to the ICU or to the Birthing Centers, she is mainly found in the Burn Centers, the Cancer Clinics, or in the Children's Ward if they have been prescreened and won't have an allergic reaction to her fur or dander. She is after all, a dog. I remember one visit in particular when a little girl was in the hospital because she had broken her back and pelvis. She couldn't sit up to see Faith so I lifted Faith up to her in her bed. She smiled and said she wanted me to put Faith down so she could practice sitting up. Her doctor said it would be a few more weeks before that happened. I promised to return. I did return and true to her word, Angela Brooke Simpson sat up in her bed and leaned over to pet my little yellow dog. Her nurses told me that she had pictures of Faith from the website taped to her bed, her wall, her tray and her bathroom door, it was her one motivation and she used it to the best of her ability! I'm never surprised what can happen, just pleased that it does happen, and when I go home with the little mutt sitting next to me on the seat in the car, I ask her if she has any idea what she's just done. I don't think she knows.

# Chapter Eighteen

## A Day in the Life of My Dog Faith

I have to laugh every time a film crew comes to my house and wants to film my dog's life. They want to capture on film for the whole world to see, the most amazing dog and all the eventful things that she must be doing during the day. Surely, they say, she must have an amazing life—well, when we're traveling she has an amazing life. I can tell you without doubt however, that at this very moment as I am writing this book my very famous, one-of-a-kind dog is laying under my bed, probably shredding the lining from under the bed, and gnawing on the baseboards. I have had to replace a couple of them so that the weight of the bed won't cause them to break when she's under it. She spends about 14-16 hours a day under the bed, and about 6 hours at night on top of it. That doesn't leave much time for much else really. She goes outside to pee, to poo, to check out the neighbor on either side, maybe to take a little walk if it's cool enough, but for the most part the dog lies under the bed all day long.

Placing the camera under the bed and watching Faith breathe and sleep wouldn't make much of a television special. The producers know this and shoot their film showing her walking through parks, chasing other dogs, playing with children, and going to the local

Starbucks. Sometimes we take treks to the library, the pet store, and we even take her to outdoor restaurants sometimes, so that's a real event. Faith's real day-in-a-life story is more like that of every other dog in the world probably. She sleeps, eats, watches television sometimes, goes back to sleep, walks around the neighborhood, goes back to sleep, and then, when it's time to come out from under the bed and go on a trip . . . that's a different story.

Faith has no problems coming out from under the bed when we say "Let's go Dog", if we just call her name she usually stays under the bed. We have discovered that saying "Let's go Dog" usually gets a faster reaction. She watches us load up the luggage and she has an idea that soon we'll be taking off, she's more than willing to do so when we call, but more than willing to stay under the bed if we don't. To Faith a ride in the car more often than not leads to a trip on an airplane, so when we just take her to the vet or the local pet store she almost feels cheated. We have actually taken her to the airport a few times just so she can think she's been somewhere. We have literally walked her through the Oklahoma City Will Rogers World Airport on dry runs on more than a dozen occasions so that she feels that she has achieved a day's work. We let her be seen by her public, we let her walk the moving sidewalks, go up the escalators, around the security check for no reason whatsoever, and then we go home. She's happy, the people at the airport are happy, and we don't actually have to fly anywhere. Matrix is so much easier to please. If I jingle the leash and harness that he walks with, he knows he's going to be going around the neighborhood four or five times. He may or may not get to go for a ride in the car, but even then just a quick trip to Target is good enough for Matrix. He's ready to go home in a few minutes, and he's had his fill of adventure that will last him for days. By the way, a day-in-the-life for Matrix is NOT under the bed, it is on top of the couch, again 14 hours a day, and then about 6 on top of the bed at night, but under the covers, where Faith doesn't like to be covered up. I am the lucky one that actually gets to share my bed with these two. It wouldn't matter if I had a twin-sized bed, full, queen, or king, I get 14 inches of sleeping space where I am allowed to turn over if I can. They take over the rest of the bed and refuse to move once they have made that last dog-sigh alerting me that disturbing them would be a sin unto death, you just don't disturb the dog once the sigh has taken place. I'm sure you understand what I'm talking about if you are a dog lover. I have had over forty years of training personally, and I know how to behave and would never consider upsetting the dog. The only time this routine is interrupted is during a storm when my duties increase, and I must become the protector. We have an agreement actually, I protect my dogs from weather, and they protect me from the Chihuahuas and the cat.

# Chapter Nineteen

What Others Had to Say

I'm going to literally copy a few stories off of the internet from places that have reported Faith's story so that the reader can understand from the point of view of others, what it is about Faith that makes her so amazing.

## From Dogs Only: Standing Ovation: True stories of an amazing biped dog called Faith and her family.

"Every now and then we hear of an amazing story that we never forget; the story of Faith is one of those remarkable tales that will leave you astonished and smiling. Faith has learned to stand and walk on her two back legs like a human. On the face of it, it's not all that unusual to see a dog stand up to greet their loved ones, or even to raise up to beg for a treat, but Faith remains upright and actually gets around this way. She may be the worlds first and only biped canine.

Faith, who suffers from a birth defect, became a member of the Stringfellow family of Oklahoma City when she was just a three-week old puppy. Puppies like Faith are rarely rescued and given a chance, but the Stringfellow family is remarkable in their own right. From the moment they first set eyes on Faith they were ready and willing to put in the time, effort and expense to take care of her. "We taught her to stand up in the snow. When she did, her legs got stronger and she just ran across and started walking," said guardian, Laura Stringfellow

Teaching Faith to stand upright wasn't the only challenge faced by Faith and her family. Because Faith's front legs were mere vestiges of what they should have been, they began to atrophy and die. Faith had to undergo surgery to remove them.

Jude Stringfellow reports, "Faith went to the doctor today. He is really very kind to her. She has extra skin over her back and neck, and it is producing fluid into the area where her leg used to be. Her shoulder is producing some of the fluid as well. He drained it, it was not infectious, so he just wrapped it tightly with a really cute stretch gauze and told her not to pull it off . . . again. She doesn't like it, but it needs to put pressure on the area. She is balancing better this week than she did last week, so we assume she will be up and running as they say, in no time."

Faith has become quite a celebrity in recent months and was scheduled to appear on the Today Show. Unfortunately, the appearance was cancelled due to the blackout in New York City.

Faith is also a Big Dog, representing Big Dog Sports in Santa Barbara, California. Says Jude: 'She has been given special treatment due to her celebrity status. They are going to let her run with the pack in the spring!'"

## From the BBC—September 4, 2006
Potter Film Hope for Disabled Dog

A two-legged dog that has learned to walk like a human could be considered for a role in the next Harry Potter film, according to reports. Faith's owners in Oklahoma City in the US believe the part could involve her appearing as the result of a spell. But the Stringfellow family said British trainers working on the film had not yet confirmed a part for Faith, who was born with the disability. The three-foot tall dog even has her own showbiz lawyer. Faith has been featured on the Ricki Lake show in the US and has attracted widespread interest from newspapers all over the world.

## Skateboard

The family has been contacted about the possibility of doing a few scenes in the fourth Harry Potter movie, The Goblet Of Fire, currently being filmed in the UK, but no plans have been finalized, they said. The 19-month-old Labrador-Chow cross was adopted by the Stringfellows as a three-week old puppy in danger of being rejected by her mother and put down. She was suffering from a birth defect that meant her front legs were not fully formed. Over six months the family taught her to stand, hop and eventually walk and run on her two back legs. Part of her therapy included being put on a skateboard to experience movement, the Stringfellows told a US newspaper. When her partial front legs began to weaken and die she had an operation to have them removed.

## From KFOR-TV Oklahoma City, OK June 23, 2003
## A dog tale deserving of a 'Standing Ovation'

"Sometimes you run across stories that leave you scratching your head. Well, we have just such a tale, one you might just have to see to believe. And, it's all about an Oklahoma City dog. But this is no ordinary dog. "She eats a lot and she plays. She's really spoiled," said her owner, Laura Stringfellow. Meet Faith. All dog. Except for one thing.

"She's very incredible," Stringfellow said. Faith walks upright, like a human.

"We got her when she was three weeks old. Her legs weren't fully developed," Stringfellow said. So Faith, not knowing any differently, started walking upright on the two strong legs she had. "We taught her to stand up in the snow. When she did, her legs got stronger and she just ran across and started walking," Stringfellow said.

And she hasn't stopped since. "We thank the Lord," she said. Faith was given to the family as a gift, and Stringfellow never thought about returning her. "When I move out, she's definitely coming with me," she said. Faith is still a pup, just 7-months-old, but full of spunk. She chases cats with the best of them."

## END

These are three of hundreds of stories about Faith that can be found on line by going to Google, or I suppose any search engine, and using the keywords "Faith the dog", or "Faith the Two-Legged Dog", literally hundreds of stories pop up. We sometimes find ourselves searching the Net just to find new stories, or to read the older ones when we find the time to do so. It still gives me a good feeling to know that so many people are writing about and thinking about my little dog. She's definitely an inspiration to me, and because of all of the evidence I can find online, I know she is touching lives all over the world.

# Chapter Twenty

## Tell About the Time Faith . . . .

Chased the geese into the lake: Faith was about six months old the first time we took her to the park and let her see geese and ducks. We weren't really sure what she would think about them, so we held on tight to her collar and let her nose her way up to them slowly. There was nothing slow about it. Faith pulled at the leash so hard she managed to slip out of her collar and headed straight for a group of big, fat, honking Canadian geese. She wanted to chase them into the water. Faith, for her part, didn't stop and think about the fact that she had no legs. Her left leg was still attached to her body, but it was behind her, and she had never been able to use it to walk or run with. I don't know what she was thinking when she ran right into the water and kept running—water splashing, geese flapping, wings and waves everywhere!

Soon after she managed to get herself into the water and up to her neck in trouble, Faith slowly turned around and saw Laura frantically waving at her—still holding the leash in her hands. Laura immediately dropped the leash and ran into the water, which was a little over her waist, and pulled Faith to the shore. Faith couldn't stop laughing. She had her mouth wide open, tongue out, and she began to push her body forward like a little mermaid. Laura instinctively let her go and there, for the first time, we saw what it looks like when Faith decides to swim. It certainly isn't pretty, I can tell you that. She throws her head in under the water and pushes back against the water with her two strong back legs, almost like the sea lions we see at the zoo. She didn't turn upside down and coast in the water like they do. She just wiggled and maneuvered her body like they do until she was fully swimming on her own. It wasn't very far, but it was on her own. She was able to swim and we didn't have to worry any longer as to whether she would truly be in trouble if she ever tried chasing geese and ducks into the water again. Which of course, she does every chance she gets. We have always assumed her father had a bit of Labrador in him.

Tell about the time Faith . . . . stopped a man from getting hit by a car. Faith was doing what she always does, just walking around on her back legs and smiling to the people she sees when suddenly—out of no where—a man popped up behind her and scared the living daylights out her. She darted away from me and ran across the parking lot with the leash dangling in the wind. I ran after her. A second man that was about to step off the curb to cross the street to where we were, decided to stay where he was. It's a good thing he did too, because a car came squealing around the corner into the parking lot we were running across. The man standing at the crosswalk would have been hit for sure. His surprise at seeing Faith may have saved his life.

Tell about the time Faith . . . went to the Atlantic Ocean. We were filming a show called Animal Attractions for Pine Ridge TV in Jacksonville, Florida. It is an episode (#102) for the new PBS-TV show Animal Attractions, and it really was a lot of fun. First the crew had to fly us to Jacksonville, Florida and then they rented us a car. Just before we were to return to the airport with the car and go home the girls wanted to drive all over the city of Jacksonville, see how many Starbucks we could find, and go to the beach. Neither Laura nor Caity had been to the ocean in several years and they hadn't been to the beaches on the north end of Florida at all. The last time they went to the ocean was when they were about seven and eight years old and they were much further south. They wanted to see if the sand was the same, if the piers were the same, if the shops and boats looked the same. I had not been to the Atlantic ocean at all, only the Pacific and I had not been to it since I was single, without children, and living in Hollywood, California working as a stand up comedian. This was going to be really fun. Faith was going to see her first ocean.

When we got in the car and drove down the highway we knew we were going in the right direction but it just seemed so far away. Ten, eleven, twelve miles from where we had started out and we thought we were a lot closer to the shoreline. Faith began to whine and we comforted her with a few *Cheez-it* crackers that we had from the flight a couple of days before. Finally, I could see a Joe's Crab Shack restaurant, and a street called 1st Avenue. If a street is called 1st Avenue chances are a street that could be called Zero Avenue would be the waterfront! It was! We parked our car and got out of it and immediately, as I closed my door, it began to rain. Buckets of rain. Fast, free-falling, bigger-than-your-fist size raindrops that seemed to smash into us rather than land gently on us as we tried making our way to the water. We were determined. Faith wasn't going to get to see the ocean every day of her life. So what if she was wet from the top as well as from the bottom, perhaps her personal experience of what it was like differs from what we think of, after all ducks like the rain. Seagulls in this case.

Seagulls were everywhere, flying in and swooping down to catch the little fish that were beginning to surface. To Faith this was an opportunity to run up and down the sand trying to catch one before it could fly up higher into the air to escape her grasp. I'm not sure what she would have done with a seagull if she had caught one, but we never had to worry about that happening. They were far faster in the air than she was on the sand, and with the rain bouncing off her like wet little bullets, the birds were fine.

Soon after it began, the rain stopped. Just stopped. Within minutes we were walking along the shoreline of the beach picking up shells and collecting little pieces of what we determined to be prehistoric creatures. I'm sure they were just bone fragments of fish that weren't as lucky as the seagulls. We found a massive cluster of shells attached to a rock but we didn't want to bring it back to Oklahoma with us because believe it or not it scared Faith. She bit at it, ran from it, barked at it, pushed it around . . . at first I thought a crab lived inside of it, but it was just something that she didn't like. A really cute couple from Argentina were honeymooning in Florida and they came running up the beach toward us. We were almost completely alone that day except for the seagulls, a pretty blond lady that ran no matter what the weather, and a couple of people from Joe's Crab Shack who had seen Faith waltzing up and down with the birds.

When the couple, Julia and Max Tanzie found us they were all giddy, laughing and carrying on. They looked very much like the couples you see in the commercials about beach vacations. They were beautiful, young, in love, they were happy, they were going to be spending the rest of their lives together—and they recognized Faith. Faith was in a commercial or an advertisement in their country. I don't speak any other language than English, and their English was a bit broken, but their smiles said all they needed to say. "This is Faith?" they asked. I said yes, and they pet her, laughed, and said something about her being on their television a month or so before. I told them about the PBS special, but I don't know if they will be able to see it in Argentina or not. Perhaps they saw Faith on Ripley's, as I know it is televised in every country that has a television station.

The hours ticked by and we had to go back to the hotel. The sand followed us all the way home from Florida. It was in our shoes, our clothes, our suitcase. In fact, when we took the car back we were a bit embarrassed to say that we had managed to get it so dirty with the sand from the beach. The attendant laughed and said it was OK, she hadn't been to the beach in several weeks and this made her feel closer to it. What a nice lady. The pictures we took of Faith at the beach are more family type photos. They don't have the resolution necessary to be printed in a book. Even though they aren't included in the book, you can close your eyes and see her running in and out of the cool water trying to catch up with the dipping white birds who wanted to catch her as much as she wanted to catch them.

Tell about the time Faith . . . went to church. Faith goes to church with me as often as I can remember to bring her, and usually during the evening hours or on a Wednesday night service when there isn't such a crowd. I would rather take her when the people aren't dressed in fine clothes that they would have to worry about getting famous yellow dog hair on. I realize that Faith is the coolest dog in the world, but some people might still be concerned about looking their best after services when they go to lunch with their families. Faith goes to our church, Metropolitan Baptist Church, but she's not a member. In order to be a member of a Baptist church you have to be a believer in Christ. Where I believe Faith is a believer, she has never actually made a profession of her beliefs, therefore, she is not a candidate for church membership. At times when we attend services Faith will become quite bored and decide it's time to walk around the halls. I usually exit the doors at that time and drive home, but there was this one time that we didn't do that at all. We were praying and I didn't notice that Faith had become disenchanted with our lengthy prayer time. She had disappeared and not one of us in the classroom actually saw her leave.

The church doors are usually closed, so there was no worry about Faith walking out of the church itself and getting into a parking lot or into someone else's car to go home. She was however interrupting a class just down the hall; you could hear the cheering, the laughing, the clapping, and the high-pitched comments of the people from that room as she made her uninvited entrance. She became an honorary member of their class, and was told that she could visit any time she felt led to do so. That's my dog, always making new friends wherever she goes.

Tell about the time Faith . . . went fishing. Faith likes to chase geese, as I've mentioned, but she also likes to bite at the little fish in the ponds we go to. There's one pond in particular that has a really interesting water display. In the Will Rogers Park in Oklahoma City, there is a pond with a couple of bridges, pretty landscaping, and an area that I swear houses water-rats or small beaver. I'm not sure what lives beneath the water, but there are certainly large koi fish and smaller minnow type fish that surface near the edge of the water. Normally, a dog probably isn't suppose to be sticking its head into the water and bobbing for minnows, but Faith does from time to time when we visit the rose garden section of that park. Each spring the rose garden has some of the most stunning specimens of roses, each labeled and marked off so that a person would be able to know the exact type of flower. Just off to the side is the picturesque pond with the floating, ever-so-beautiful koi and their little friends the shiny, silvery little minnows that bob up and down, swim sideways and even wiggle a bit—almost inviting little yellow dogs to poke at them with their curious noses. Faith can resist. Faith doesn't try to resist. Faith is a dog. PLOP! There went the head, straight under the water, up she came with a mouthful of wiggling, squirming, shiny, silvery little minnows. None of us could catch her before she swallowed them whole.

Tell about the time Faith . . . surprised the newlyweds. We were staying at the Amerisuites Hotel in Grapevine, Texas on our trip where we performed at the Texas Outdoor Expo this past summer. Caroline, the lady at the front desk who absolutely loves my dog, told me that a newlywed couple had come in the night before and had seen Faith and I in the Business Center. Not wishing to disturb us, they asked Caroline about Faith, and she was able to tell them a few things about her; where we lived, how old Faith was, what had happened to her legs, that sort of stuff. The next morning before we took off for the show, Faith hung back with Laura in the room while I ate breakfast. When Laura pushed the elevator button to come downstairs she noticed that Faith had taken off down the hall and was going into a room that a maid had opened just a few feet away from the elevator that she obviously didn't want to wait for. The couple was sound asleep in their bed, and the maid was a bit embarrassed that she had opened the door. Trying to back out of the room was hard enough for the woman, but to try and call Faith from it was impossible. Laura shot down the hall as quickly as she could, and from outside the room began calling to Faith to come out. Faith had other plans. She thought the couple looked nice enough to talk to, and they were just waking up, so they wouldn't mind scratching the head of a little intruder, maybe they had food nearby. The bride laughed first and then her husband, both said they'd be down to breakfast as soon as they could, and they wanted to take pictures with Faith if possible. I'm not saying every honeymoon should include being awakened by a friendly furry face, but it may be a great way to start out a new life together.

Tell about the time Faith . . . went to college. I have been a professor of English and an English teacher. I prefer to teach people who prefer to learn, so often times I would bring my dog to school to show the students that if I can make a dog walk upright, I can certainly guarantee that they will get their homework completed on time. One of the colleges I taught at was Oklahoma City Community College. OKCCC, as it is called, is one of the largest community colleges in the country. I believe we had over 28,000 students signed up for the fall semester of 2005. Because OKCCC is a community college anyone and everyone attends, we have students from every walk of life, and from every age demographic known to man. In one of my classes I had students still in high school and others that were great grandparents. One of the assignments was to observe Faith, and to write out a brief outline for an essay that would best describe her to a person who could not see and could not hear. This was not an easy assignment.

Faith obliged everyone in the room by going person-to-person, or dog-to-person, and sniffing them, letting them know she wasn't going to get closer, or perhaps she wanted in their laps. She made many decisions that night. She came back to the front of the room only after she had been fed, weaseling out chips, candy, treats, even taking their water from them if they were willing to surrender it. Her method of asking for their loot was pure guilt. She'd just stare up at them, wag her tail, wimp a little, and sit right next to them until they eventually were guilted out of everything they were hiding in their backpacks. By the end of the hour anyone who could not have heard a word or seen even a ray of light would have known what it felt like to be in the room with a little scavenger that stood upright and didn't have her front legs. I almost felt sorry for some of the students who had actually given up their evening meal, but then again, that's part of life too . . . you have to say no. Faith can take it. She'll just look at you for another minute or two, but she does get told no from time to time. Probably not as often as she should, but she is at least acquainted with the term.

# Chapter Twenty-One

One Last Story, and Then I Gotta Go

Faith's future is so bright. We have been trying to find her a talent agent so that she can be seen on the big screen. We feel that she has such an amazing story that people would like to be able to see her on DVD forever, after all she is a dog and she won't live forever. We know that Faith is capable of being a dog in a show where she belongs to someone and they take her places and they do fun things with her. Often times we get calls from independent film makers that want Faith in their movies, but the movies they want to film aren't the type of movies I would want my dog to be a part of. Faith has a really cool story to tell and she tells it without any words at all.

Imagine yourself under a tree somewhere, maybe reading a book or a newspaper and just basically hanging out doing nothing. The weather is good, you've paid all of your bills, the kids are playing in the sandbox close by, there really isn't anything wrong in your life, but there isn't anything great going on either. Suddenly you look up and from just over the knoll you see a little dog skipping, yes, skipping on her back legs, and she's got her head up in the air nipping at what looks to be a fat little bumblebee. That second—that one second of time will never leave you. You don't know what it is, but that dog just changed everything. She doesn't have front legs. She shouldn't be alive. She shouldn't be walking upright if somehow she did manage to survive puppy-hood, but she's running after a bumblebee, and she just might catch it. That is Faith's story. Anything is possible and nothing is impossible. Never let a day go by without thinking of the bumblebee—because bumblebees can't fly either. But they do.

When Faith came into my life I was not the lady sitting under the tree without any worries. I was the single mom with three teens and/or preteen children with school bills, clothes to buy, insurance needs, you name it. I was about to be unemployed without any support from anyone when suddenly, in he came through the front door smiling at me. My son Reuben had brought me a little gift. It wasn't a very expensive gift, but this gift was going to cost me quite a bit to keep it. Eventually I would have to quit my job to train her to walk. I would have to alter my lifestyle to accommodate hers. This was going to be a very interesting ride. Looking into my son's face I saw that what he was doing was an act of kindness, of love, and what he wanted to do was incredible. He wanted to help a little defenseless dog to be able to live like any other dog—he wanted me to help him with his cause. Bumblebees don't have the capacity to fly. But they do. With a little strength, a little time, a little work, a little faith . . . they fly. And, believe it or not, some dogs walk upright on their back legs so they have a better chance at catching them. You gotta believe.

# Acknowledgements

I have a full schedule these days. I take Faith traveling and we do shows and performances where she can showcase her abilities to walk and skip, to be the dog that she was meant to be. I have three kids to raise, one went to the Army, but now I have to worry about that as well. From time to time I have to set myself and my schedule to the side and just write. It isn't easy because I write best in the mornings and I have to be a mom in the afternoons and evenings. I have errands, I have kids, I have all the normal things I have to do like you do. So, when I can find time to write I have to stop and take the necessary time it takes to thank the *three* people that left me alone long enough so that I could actually get the work done. To Reuben Andrew Stringfellow, my beautiful and brave son. I thank you. I know you are about to go into the United States Army, (Thanks Sgt. Major David Best, I won't forget you . . . *ever*) and that you will be driving big, mean, tanks in order to protect me and my little girls. I love you for your commitment, and for your pride not only in your country, but in yourself. You've really become a wonderful man. To Laura Stringfellow, my absolutely gorgeous red-headed, talented, singing and acting daughter, *who* sacrificed everything for me and my goals—*who* slept until after 3:00 p.m. each and every day just so that I could write this book. To you I will always be grateful. I want you to wake up now, and clean the house. To Caity-Baby (CBBC) Stringfellow, my littlest angel, precious, beautiful and willing to

121

run away from any and all responsibilities around the house just so I could type. You surrendered not only your time my darling, but your computer too. You are awesome. Now, get back here and straighten out the closet. (Oh, and do you have any idea where my credit card is?) Also, I want to thank Patti and Ron Hetzel of the Cleveland, Ohio area. During our trip to Cleveland this summer to do the Canine Fun Days and Greyhound Reunion, Patti and Ron brought their pretty dog Goldie, a 90 pound Lab/Retriever mix, up to the show and they sat in our tent for the entire two days answering questions and being the groupies they were meant to be. They have years of experience at being groupies, having traveled with and worked for the 60's style band *Phil Dirt and the Dozers*. Thanks for the burgers, and Patti thanks for the ice cream cones you donated to Faith over and over again.